ANNUAL REPORT 2013

Board of Governors of the Federal Reserve System, Consumer Financial Protection Bureau, Federal Deposit Insurance Corporation, National Credit Union Administration, Office of the Comptroller of the Currency, State Liaison Committee

Federal Financial Institutions Examination Council

ANNUAL REPORT 2013

Board of Governors of the Federal Reserve System, Consumer Financial Protection Bureau, Federal Deposit Insurance Corporation, National Credit Union Administration, Office of the Comptroller of the Currency, State Liaison Committee

MEMBERS OF THE COUNCIL

Richard Cordray, Director, Consumer Financial Protection Bureau; David J. Cotney, Commissioner of Banks, Commonwealth of Massachusetts; Debbie Matz, Chairman, National Credit Union Administration; Thomas J. Curry, FFIEC Chairman, Comptroller of the Currency, Office of the Comptroller of the Currency; Daniel K. Tarullo, FFIEC Vice Chairman, Member, Board of Governors of the Federal Reserve System; Martin J. Gruenberg, Chairman, Federal Deposit Insurance Corporation.

LETTER OF TRANSMITTAL

Federal Financial Institutions
   Examination Council
Arlington, VA 22226
March 28, 2014

The President of the Senate
The Speaker of the House of Representatives

Pursuant to the provisions of section 1006(f) of the Financial Institutions Regulatory and Interest Rate Control Act of 1978 (12 U.S.C. § 3305), I am pleased to submit the 2013 Annual Report of the Federal Financial Institutions Examination Council.

Respectfully,

Thomas J. Curry
Chairman

TABLE OF CONTENTS

CHART OF SELECTED ABBREVIATIONS

ALG	Agency Liaison Group
APP	Bank Financial Data Application
ASC	Appraisal Subcommittee
BHC	Bank Holding Company
BSA/AML	Bank Secrecy Act/Anti-Money Laundering
Call Report	Consolidated Reports of Condition and Income
CCIWG	Cybersecurity and Critical Infrastructure Working Group
CDR	Central Data Repository
CFPB	Consumer Financial Protection Bureau
CRA	Community Reinvestment Act of 1977
CSBS	Conference of State Bank Supervisors
DIF	Deposit Insurance Fund
Dodd-Frank Act	Dodd-Frank Wall Street Reform and Consumer Protection Act
EEO	Examiner Education Office
EGRPRA	Economic Growth and Regulatory Paperwork Reduction Act of 1996
FAQ	Frequently Asked Question
FCRA	Fair Credit Reporting Act
FDIC	Federal Deposit Insurance Corporation
FDICIA	Federal Deposit Insurance Corporation Improvement Act of 1991
FFIEC	Federal Financial Institutions Examination Council
FFIEC 101	Advanced Capital Adequacy Framework Regulatory Reporting Requirements
FFIEC 009	Country Exposure Report
FFIEC 009a	Country Exposure Information Report
FHC	Financial Holding Company
FinCEN	Financial Crimes Enforcement Network
FIRIRCA	Financial Institutions Regulatory and Interest Rate Control Act of 1978
FIRREA	Financial Institutions Reform, Recovery, and Enforcement Act of 1989
FRB	Board of Governors of the Federal Reserve System
FRS	Federal Reserve System
FSOC	Financial Stability Oversight Council
HMDA	Home Mortgage Disclosure Act of 1975
IBA	International Banking Act of 1978

ILDR	Interagency Loan Data Report
IT	Information Technology
IT Handbook	Information Technology Examination Handbook
IWG	Innovation Working Group
LAG	Legal Advisory Group
MDPS	Multi-Regional Data Processing Servicer
NCUA	National Credit Union Administration
NMLS	Nationwide Mortgage Licensing System
OCC	Office of the Comptroller of the Currency
OMB	Office of Management and Budget
PDD	Public Data Distribution
PRA	Paperwork Reduction Act of 1980
SASR	Shared Application Software Review
SDRWG	Structure Data Reconciliation Working Group
SIFIs	Systemically Important Financial Institutions
SLC	State Liaison Committee
SLHC	Savings and Loan Holding Company
SME	Subject Matter Expert
TFCC	Task Force on Consumer Compliance
TFEE	Task Force on Examiner Education
TFIS	Task Force on Information Sharing
TFOR	Task Force on Reports
TFOS	Task Force on Supervision
TFSS	Task Force on Surveillance Systems
TSP	Technology Service Provider
TWG	Technology Working Group
UBPR	Uniform Bank Performance Report
XP	Microsoft Windows XP Operating System

MESSAGE FROM THE CHAIRMAN

FFIEC Chairman Thomas J. Curry

I am pleased to report on the activities of the Federal Financial Institutions Examination Council (FFIEC or Council). This has been another productive year for the Council, its member agencies and the State Liaison Committee. In 2013, the Council continued to advance its mission of promoting uniformity and consistency in the supervision of financial institutions.

The FFIEC provided leadership on major policy initiatives that prescribe uniform principles, standards and report forms for the federal examination of financial institutions by its member agencies. The FFIEC also continued to foster communication, cooperation, and coordination among the member agencies and the State Liaison Committee, the entities that make up the Council and its task forces. To this end, the Council's 2013 activities included two notable initiatives that will continue in the coming year. In light of the growing sophistication of cyber attacks and the global importance of critical infrastructure protection, the Council formed a permanent working group as a subset of the Task Force on Supervision to serve as a forum to address policy issues regarding critical infrastructure and cybersecurity. In support of this role, the group will liaise with law enforcement and the Department of Homeland Security and will assist with the development of examination standards, training, information sharing, and industry awareness.

The Council also established an interagency group to prepare for the second decennial review of regulations required under Section 2222 of the Economic Growth and Regulatory Paperwork Reduction Act of 1996 (EGRPRA). The FFIEC and each appropriate federal banking agency are to identify regulatory requirements that may be outdated, unnecessary or unduly burdensome and, in a report to Congress, to address whether such regulatory burdens can be changed through regulation or require legislation. As with the prior EGRPRA review, opportunities to reduce burdens on community institutions will be an important focus for the Council and its member agencies.

The Council and its subcommittees and task forces were involved in a number of other important initiatives this past year. The Council's 2013 achievements are detailed later in the report. Notable accomplishments during the year include the following:

- Issued Social Media Guidance to help financial institutions understand potential risks associated with the use of social media, along with expectations for managing those risks.

- Developed interagency guidance that was issued jointly with the Federal Trade Commission, the Securities and Exchange Commission, and the Commodity Futures Trading Commission to clarify existing privacy laws and the reporting of suspected financial abuse of older adults to the appropriate state and federal agencies.

- Approved examination procedures in four areas: Truth in Lending Act (Regulation Z);

Real Estate Settlement Procedures Act (Regulation X); new garnishment requirements issued by the Treasury Department and federal benefits agencies; and remittances.

- Provided 106 sessions of courses and conferences through the Task Force on Examiner Education and the FFIEC Examiner Education Office. Approximately 3,900 federal regulatory and state supervisory agency staff received superior training on a range of industry-specific topics. The offerings included a newly developed Consumer Compliance Specialist Conference that provides examiner training on emerging issues.

- Advanced efforts to enhance the efficiency of, and technology for, facilitating the sharing of electronic information among the Council's member agencies in support of the supervision, regulation, and deposit insurance responsibilities of financial institution regulators, including changes to the Interagency Loan Data Report.

- Developed certain final and proposed revisions to the Consolidated Reports of Condition and Income (Call Report) and FFIEC reports filed by institutions, including changes to regulatory capital reporting consistent with the revised regulatory capital rules approved by the federal banking agencies during July 2013. These revisions are in various stages of completion and reflect extensive deliberations among the Council and Task Force on Reports, including the evaluation of public comments, in an effort to minimize burden on institutions where possible.

- Developed and published updated interagency guidance on the classification and appraisal of securities to implement requirements in the Dodd-Frank Wall Street Reform and Consumer Protection Act that directs the agencies to replace references to, and reliance on, credit ratings as the basis for financial institutions' classification of securities with appropriate standards of creditworthiness.

- Developed and issued a proposed addendum to interagency guidance that clarifies how certain regulatory restrictions on, and requirements for, transactions between depository institutions and their affiliates apply to tax allocation agreements in a holding company structure.

- Sponsored the annual FFIEC Information Technology Conference for examiners, which highlighted emerging technology issues and lessons learned from the impact of Superstorm Sandy on technology service providers.

- Promoted collaboration on potential enhancements to the Uniform Bank Performance Report and explored opportunities to increase the Report's usability.

I am extremely proud of the significant accomplishments that the FFIEC, its task forces, and the interagency working groups achieved in 2013. As depository institutions continue to address the challenges of a slow economy and an evolving regulatory and legislative landscape, the Council's role has become even more vital. In the coming year, the Council looks forward to continuing its efforts to work together to advance the mission of promoting uniformity and consistency in the supervision of financial institutions.

Overview of the Federal Financial Institutions Examination Council Operations

The Federal Financial Institutions Examination Council (FFIEC or Council) was established on March 10, 1979, pursuant to title X of the Financial Institutions Regulatory and Interest Rate Control Act of 1978 (FIRIRCA), Public Law 95-630. The purpose of title X, cited as the Federal Financial Institutions Examination Council Act of 1978, was to create a formal interagency body empowered to prescribe uniform principles, standards, and report forms for the federal examination of financial institutions by the constituent agencies, and to make recommendations to promote uniformity in the supervision of financial institutions. The Council is responsible for developing uniform reporting systems for federally supervised financial institutions, their holding companies, and the nonfinancial institution subsidiaries of those institutions and holding companies. It conducts schools for examiners employed by the five federal member agencies represented on the Council and makes those schools available to employees of state agencies that supervise financial institutions.

To encourage the application of uniform examination principles and standards by the state and federal supervisory authorities, the Council established, in accordance with the requirement of FIRIRCA, the State Liaison Committee (SLC).

Membership, Organization, and Administration of the Council

Members of the Council

The Council has six voting members, and in 2013 it was comprised of

- a member of the Board of Governors of the Federal Reserve System (FRB), appointed by the Chairman of the Board;

- the Chairman of the Federal Deposit Insurance Corporation (FDIC);

- the Chairman of the National Credit Union Administration (NCUA);

- the Comptroller of the Currency of the Office of the Comptroller of the Currency (OCC);

- the Director of the Consumer Financial Protection Bureau (CFPB); and

- the Chairman of the State Liaison Committee (SLC).

Interagency Task Forces and Liaisons

Six staff task forces effectively administer the full spectrum of projects in the Council's functional areas, including but not limited to researching future enhancements for reporting, examiner training products, and examiner guidance. The task forces are each composed of six senior officials, drawn from the five federal member agencies, and a representative of the SLC. Each is tasked with one of the following subject matters:

- Consumer Compliance

- Examiner Education

- Information Sharing

- Reports

- Supervision

- Surveillance Systems

The Council has a Legal Advisory Group (LAG), composed of the general or chief counsel of each member entity, to provide support to the Council and staff in the substantive areas of concern. The task forces and the LAG provide research and develop analytical papers and proposals on the issues that the Council addresses. In addition, the Council has an Agency Liaison Group, composed of senior officials responsible for coordinating the FFIEC work of their respective agencies' staff members.

Administration of the Council

The Chairmanship of the Council continuously rotates among the federal members for a two-year term in the following order: OCC, FRB, FDIC, CFPB, and NCUA. The Council holds regular meetings at least twice a year. Other Council meetings may be convened whenever called by the Chairman or four or more Council members. The Council's activities are funded in several ways. Most of the Council's funds are derived from assessments on its five federal member agencies. It receives tuition fees from non-agency attendees to cover some of the costs associated with its examiner education program.

In 2013, the FRB continued to provide budget and accounting services to the Council. The Council is supported by a small, full-time administrative staff in its operations office and in its examiner education program, which are located at the FDIC's L. William

Seidman Center in Arlington, Virginia. Each Council staff is detailed (some permanently) from one of the five federal member agencies represented on the Council.

A Brief Statutory History of the Council

The Financial Institutions Regulatory and Interest Rate Control Act of 1978

Upon passage of the Financial Institutions Regulatory and Interest Rate Control Act of 1978, the constituent agencies each designated personnel to study title X, analyze the agencies' responsibilities, and prepare recommendations for performing the required duties. The heads of the constituent agencies, acting through the Interagency Coordinating Committee, then established a task force composed of representatives from each agency to develop the necessary mechanism to establish the Council. The task force prepared option papers and legal opinions for the Council on organization structure, rules of operation, funding, priorities, and other necessary matters pertinent to the establishment of a functioning Council. The Council organized and held its first meeting on March 16, 1979. At the first meeting of the Council, the organizations were represented by John G. Heimann, Comptroller of the Currency of the OCC; Irvine H. Sprague, Chairman of the FDIC; J. Charles Partee, Governor of the FRB; Robert H. McKinney, Chairman of the Federal Home Loan Bank Board (Bank Board); and Lawrence Connell, Administrator of the NCUA.

The Housing and Community Development Act of 1980

The Council was given additional statutory responsibilities by section 340 of the Housing and Community Development Act of 1980, Public Law 96-399. Among these responsibilities are the implementation of a system to facilitate public access to data that depository institutions must disclose under the Home Mortgage Disclosure Act of 1975 (HMDA) and the aggregation of annual HMDA data, by census tract, for each metropolitan statistical area.

The Financial Institutions Reform, Recovery, and Enforcement Act of 1989

In 1989, the Financial Institutions Reform, Recovery, and Enforcement Act (FIRREA) abolished the Federal Home Loan Bank Board and established the Office of Thrift Supervision (OTS). Accordingly, the Director of the OTS assumed the Council seat previously held by the Bank Board representative.

Title XI of FIRREA established the Appraisal Subcommittee (ASC) within the Council. The ASC's mission statement is "to provide federal oversight of State appraiser regulatory programs and a monitoring framework for the Appraisal Foundation and the Federal Financial Institutions Regulatory Agencies in their roles to protect federal financial and public policy interests in real estate appraisals utilized in federally related transactions." The ASC consists of seven individuals appointed by the heads of the five federal regulatory agencies represented on the Council and the Federal Housing Finance Agency and the U.S. Department of Housing and Urban Development. The ASC is largely autonomous and performs its duties independently of the direct supervision and oversight of the Council. The Council's responsibilities with respect to the ASC include: (1) selection of the chairman of the ASC; (2) approval of any adjustment of the amount of the ASC's annual registry fee for appraisers that exceeds the statutorily-defined amount; (3) approval of any determination by the ASC to waive any certification or licensing requirement based on a scarcity of appraisers in connection with federally related transactions within a state; and (4) approval of any proposal by the ASC to grant extensions to states to comply with new regulations governing establishment of appraisal management company registration and supervision systems.

The Economic Growth and Regulatory Paperwork Reduction Act of 1996

Additional responsibility was given to the Council by the Economic Growth and Regulatory Paperwork Reduction Act of 1996 (EGRPRA) to submit reports to Congress on the regulatory reviews that its constituent agencies, with the exception of the NCUA, and with the later exception of the CFPB, conduct in accordance with EGRPRA.

The EGRPRA requires that the constituent agencies, at least once every 10 years, review all the regulations prescribed by the agencies to identify those that are outdated or otherwise impose unnecessary regulatory requirements on insured depository institutions and eliminate unnecessary regulations. Although not required to, the NCUA elects to participate in the decennial review process. CFPB is required to complete a review of each significant rule five years after it takes effect, in a process separate from EGRPRA.

The Financial Services Regulatory Relief Act of 2006

Congress passed the Financial Services Regulatory Relief Act of 2006 that provided for the election of a Chairman for the SLC from among the five SLC members and for the addition of the SLC Chairman as a voting member of the Council in October 2006.

The Secure and Fair Enforcement for Mortgage Licensing Act of 2008

The Secure and Fair Enforcement for Mortgage Licensing Act of 2008 (SAFE Act), enacted as title V of the Housing and Economic Recovery Act of 2008, established the responsibility for the federal banking agencies, through the Council and in conjunction with the Farm Credit Administration, to develop and maintain a system for registering employees of depository institutions and certain of their subsidiaries' loan originators with the Nationwide Mortgage Licensing System (NMLS) and Registry. On July 21, 2011, pursuant to the Dodd-Frank Wall Street Reform and Consumer Protection Act (Dodd-Frank Act), the authority for rulemaking and authority to develop and maintain the NMLS generally was transferred to the CFPB.

The Dodd-Frank Wall Street Reform and Consumer Protection Act of 2010

In 2010, Congress enacted the Dodd-Frank Act, providing for the addition of the Director of the CFPB as a voting member of the Council, effective July 2011. The Director of the OTS was removed from the Council, and the agency's functions were transferred to the OCC, FRB, FDIC, and CFPB.

RECORD OF COUNCIL ACTIVITIES

The Federal Financial Institutions Examination Council in session.

The following section is a chronological record of the official actions taken by the FFIEC during 2013, pursuant to the Federal Financial Institutions Examination Council Act of 1978, as amended, and the HMDA, as amended.

February 4, 2013

Action. Approved the issuance of the Council's annual interagency awards.

Explanation. The Council has an interagency awards program that recognizes individuals of the member agencies who have provided outstanding service to the Council on interagency projects and programs during the previous year.

March 8, 2013

Action. Approved the appointment of six task force chairs.

Explanation. The chairs for all six standing task forces are approved annually and are drawn from management and staff of the five federal member agencies and representatives of the SLC.

March 8, 2013

Action. Approved the 2012 annual report of the Council to the Congress.

Explanation. The legislation establishing the Council requires that, not later than April 1 of each year,

the Council publish an annual report covering its activities during the preceding year.

April 11, 2013

Action. Approved appointment of new SLC member, Karen K. Lawson, Office of Banking, Michigan Department of Insurance and Financial Services.

Explanation. The Council appoints two of the SLC members. The remaining three members are designated by the Conference of State Bank Supervisors, the American Council of State Savings Supervisors, and the National Association of State Credit Union Supervisors.

FFIEC Chairman Curry addressing the Council at a 2013 meeting. Pictured to the right is FDIC Chairman Gruenberg.

Development, vacated this position before his term expired. Arthur W. Lindo was approved to serve as the Chair for the remaining months of this two-year term, which expires on March 31, 2014.

June 6, 2013

Action. Approved the formation of the FFIEC Cybersecurity and Critical Infrastructure Working Group (CCIWG).

Explanation. The Council approved the formation of the CCIWG to be a permanent working group under the Task Force on Supervision (TFOS) to address the need for coordination across the member agencies on cybersecurity and critical infrastructure.

November 22, 2013

Action. Approved the revised Rules of Operations, Resolutions, and Task Force Charters.

Explanation. With the passage of the Dodd-Frank Act, revisions to the Council's founding documents were necessary to reflect the current membership of the Council and each task force. Thus, references to the OTS were removed, and the role of the CFPB was added. These revisions went into effect on December 3, 2013.

December 4, 2013

Action. Approved the 2014 Council budget.

Explanation. The Council is required to approve the annual budget that funds the Council's staff, programs, and activities.

May 15, 2013

Action. Approved a revised HMDA MOU by and between the FFIEC member agencies and the Federal Reserve Board (FRB) regarding HMDA reports.

Explanation. The HMDA MOU was developed in response to one of the findings of an internal FFIEC operations review that was presented to the Council in 2002. The MOU outlines the responsibilities that the FRB performs related to HMDA data that are collected by member agencies from financial institutions required to file HMDA reports and reflects the changes necessitated from the passage of the Dodd-Frank Act, including the addition of the CFPB as a party to the MOU, and removal of the OTS from the MOU.

May 15, 2013

Action. Approved a revised Community Reinvestment Act (CRA) MOU.

Explanation. The CRA MOU was updated to reflect the changes necessitated from the passage of the Dodd-Frank Act, including the removal of the OTS from the MOU.

June 6, 2013

Action. Approved selection of the ASC Chair, Arthur W. Lindo, FRB.

Explanation. The Council is required to approve the selection of the ASC Chair, who serves a two-year term. Previous Chair, Peter W. Gillispie, U.S. Department of Housing and Urban

STATE LIAISON COMMITTEE REPORT

State Liaison Committee (from left to right): Thomas Candon (VT), Lauren Kingry (AZ), David Cotney (MA), Michael Mach (WI), and Karen Lawson (MI).

The State Liaison Committee (SLC) consists of five representatives from state regulatory agencies that supervise financial institutions. The representatives are appointed for two-year terms. An SLC member may have his or her two-year term extended by the appointing organization for an additional, consecutive two-year term. Each year, the SLC elects one of its members to serve as chairman for 12 months. David J. Cotney, Commissioner of Banks of the Commonwealth of Massachusetts Division of Banks, is serving as the current chairman of the SLC. The Council elects two of the five members of the SLC. The American Council of State Savings Supervisors, the Conference of State Bank Supervisors (CSBS), and the National Association of State Credit Union Supervisors each designate a member. The members of the SLC serve as an important conduit to their state colleagues and represent state supervisory interests before the Council.

The SLC is represented on the Council's task forces and working groups by state supervisors from around the country. The CSBS provides staff support to the SLC representatives and serves as the primary liaison to the FFIEC staff for all administrative matters.

In connection with its role on the Council, the SLC meets in person before each Council meeting to review the agenda and discuss topics of interest which may come before the Council. The SLC welcomes leadership and policymakers from the FFIEC member agencies to meet with them during these briefings to engage in informal dialogue. Those who participated this year included Thomas J. Curry, Chairman, FFIEC, Comptroller of the Currency, OCC; Debbie Matz, Chairman, NCUA; and Judith E. Dupre, Executive Secretary, FFIEC.

ACTIVITIES OF THE INTERAGENCY STAFF TASK FORCES

Task Force on Consumer Compliance

The Task Force on Consumer Compliance promotes policy coordination, a common supervisory approach, and uniform enforcement of consumer protection laws and regulations. The task force identifies and analyzes emerging consumer compliance issues and develops proposed policies and procedures to foster consistency among the agencies. Additionally, the task force reviews legislation, regulations, and policies at the state and federal level that may have a bearing on the compliance responsibilities of the member agencies.

During 2013, the task force relied on the HMDA/CRA Data Collection Subcommittee and several ad hoc working groups to carry out its mission. The task force meets monthly to address and resolve common issues in compliance supervision. While significant issues or recommendations are referred to the Council for action, the Council has delegated to the task force the authority to make certain decisions and recommendations.

Initiatives Addressed in 2013

Social Media Guidance

The task force formed a working group to draft guidance on consumer compliance issues related to social media, culminating in the approval of the Social Media Guidance, after a public comment period, at the September 12, 2013, task force meeting. The working group collaborated with the Infor-

Task Force on Consumer Compliance meeting.

mation Technology Subcommittee of the Task Force on Supervision on specifics within the Guidance, which was released on December 11, 2013. The agencies held an interagency webinar aimed at industry participants to discuss the Guidance in December 2013.

HMDA/CRA Data Collection Subcommittee Activities

The 2012 CRA and HMDA data were processed and aggregated, and were released to the public on September 18, 2013, through the FFIEC Website, www.ffiec. gov/press/pr091813.htm. The 2012 HMDA data are the first to use the census tract delineations and population and housing characteristic data from the 2010 Census and from the American Community Survey.

Additionally, the 2014 budget for HMDA and CRA data process-

ing was approved by the task force during its September 10, 2013, meeting and was part of the overall budget package approved by the Council at its December 4, 2013, meeting. In January 2013, the task force convened a working group to review and revise the HMDA and CRA content on the FFIEC Website. This working group developed two product enhancements: a new geocoding system and the addition of an Excel format for HMDA/CRA Aggregate and Disclosure Reports. Both proposals were approved by the task force, and then by the Council as part of the 2014 HMDA and CRA data processing budget.

Mortgage Rules Examination Procedures

Under the Dodd-Frank Act, the CFPB was required to issue new mortgage rules by January 21,

2013. Most of the rules have a January 2014 effective date, and the task force convened an interagency effort, led by the CFPB, to draft examination procedures covering these new rules. To date, the task force has approved three sets of examination procedures and various technical updates covering later regulatory changes. Two sets of procedures for Truth in Lending Act (TILA)/Regulation Z changes were approved June 5 and August 8, 2013, and procedures for Real Estate Settlement Procedures Act (RESPA)/Regulation X were approved August 9, 2013. On November 14, 2013, the task force approved technical updates to both the TILA and RESPA examination procedures.

Consumer Compliance Specialists Conference

In 2013, the task force continued to collaborate with the Task Force on Examiner Education and the FFIEC Examiner Education Office (EEO) to develop and plan the Consumer Compliance Specialists Conference. The conference addresses supervisory updates and emerging issues for experienced examiners. The program was originally offered in January 2013, and after positive feedback, was offered again in October 2013. Planning is under way for an April 2014 offering.

Elder Financial Abuse Bulletin

On September 24, 2013, the FFIEC agencies, along with the Federal Trade Commission, Commodity Futures Trading Commission, and the Securities and Exchange Commission, issued an Elder Financial Abuse Bulletin. The Bulletin clarifies existing laws regarding the reporting of suspected financial abuse of older adults to appropriate state or federal agencies, explaining that this does not, in general, violate the privacy provi-

sions of the Gramm-Leach-Bliley Act or its implementing regulation, Regulation P.

Garnishment Rule Examination Procedures

The task force formed a working group to develop examination procedures to be used by the agencies to evaluate depository institutions' compliance with the garnishment rule issued by the Treasury Department and federal benefits agencies. Finalized on May 29, 2013, the Treasury Department rule requires financial institutions to take steps to alleviate the hardship experienced by account holders who receive certain types of federal benefits when the garnishment process occurs. The task force approved procedures based on the interim final rule on May 9, 2013, and approved final procedures on August 19, 2013.

Remittance Transfer Rule Examination Procedures

The task force formed a working group to develop examination procedures to assess compliance with the new remittance rule issued pursuant to section 1073 of the

Dodd-Frank Act, which amends Regulation E, which implements the Electronic Fund Transfer Act. The task force approved the procedures on August 8, 2013.

Task Force on Examiner Education

The Task Force on Examiner Education oversees the FFIEC's examiner education program on behalf of the Council. The task force promotes interagency education through timely, cost-efficient, state-of-the-art training programs for federal and state examiners and agency staff. The task force develops programs on its own initiative and in response to requests from the Council, Council task forces, and suggestions brought forth by the EEO staff. The EEO also maintains development groups that have been established to provide ongoing content guidance for classes and conferences. Development group members consist of subject matter experts (SMEs) from each FFIEC member entity designated by their task force members. Development group members help the EEO

Task Force on Examiner Education meeting.

Instructor Thomas deRoque facilitates group work during FFIEC's Advanced Commercial Credit Analysis class at FDIC's L. William Seidman Center, Arlington, VA.

ensure that the course content is relevant, current, and meeting the agencies' training needs.

Each fall, EEO staff prepares a training calendar based on demand from the FFIEC member entities and state financial institution regulators, which is then approved by the task force. The EEO staff schedules, delivers, and evaluates training programs throughout the year.

Initiatives Addressed in 2013

The task force has continued to ensure that the FFIEC's educational programs meet the needs of agency personnel, are cost-effective, and are widely available. The task force meets monthly with the EEO staff to discuss emerging topics, to review feedback from each course and conference, and to develop a framework for future courses and conferences. The solid partnership between the task force principals and the EEO staff promotes open and regular communication that continues to result in high-quality, well-received training.

In 2013, the EEO administered 106 task force sponsored training sessions, with a total of 3,903 attendees (see table on the following page for attendee participation by program and entity). Highlights from this year's training initiatives include the following:

Two Consumer Compliance Specialists Conferences were held in

2013 with 281 attendees overall.

In response to changes in supervision responsibilities outlined in the Dodd-Frank Act, the EEO split the Supervisory Updates and Emerging Issues Conferences into two separate conferences—one for Community Financial Institutions and the other for Large, Complex Financial Institutions. This specific breakdown enabled the examiners to focus on those emerging topics most applicable to the banks they examine.

The EEO held its first "paperless" conference for the annual Information Technology (IT) Conference in September, which was well received. The EEO also provided support for an IT Symposium held in October on the chosen topic, "Strengthening the Resilience of Outsourced Technology Service Providers." The IT Symposium is an initiative under the Task Force on Supervision's IT Subcommittee that includes one week of presentations from industry experts and additional weeks dedicated to the development of a work product. The development of the program for the first week

Thomas Curry, FFIEC Chairman, Comptroller of the Currency (OCC), addresses attendees at the FFIEC's Consumer Compliance Specialists Conference at the FDIC's L. William Seidman Center Hove Auditorium.

2013 Participation in FFIEC Training by Program and Entity-Actual as of December 31, 2013

Program Title	FRB	FRB State Sponsored	FDIC	FDIC State Sponsored	NCUA	OCC	CFPB	FCA	FHFA	Other	Total
Advanced BSA/AML Specialists Conference	24	7	36	12	3	29	3	0	0	12	126
Advanced Commercial Credit Analysis	16	9	27	8	9	25	0	2	0	0	96
Anti-Money Laundering Workshop	14	13	50	12	8	0	2	1	0	8	108
Asset Management Forum	29	12	67	17	0	17	0	0	0	0	142
Advanced Cash Flow Concepts & Analysis: Beyond the Numbers	33	9	46	0	9	30	1	3	5	0	136
Capital Markets Conference	28	24	72	14	20	10	5	3	8	0	184
Capital Markets Specialists Conference	42	4	87	12	7	18	2	11	5	0	188
Cash Flow Construction and Analysis from Federal Tax Returns	34	23	100	17	20	50	0	3	0	1	248
Commercial Real Estate Analysis	51	23	119	32	16	29	0	2	4	7	283
Consumer Compliance Specialists Conference	26	4	77	0	30	29	112	0	0	3	281
Distressed Commercial Real Estate	34	7	126	19	17	17	0	0	0	0	220
Financial Crimes Seminar	34	8	144	10	9	22	0	0	1	5	233
Fraud Identification Training Online	2	0	20	0	1	6	9	0	0	0	38
Fraud Investigation Techniques for Examiners	6	3	16	0	20	5	3	0	0	1	54
Fundamentals of Fraud Workshop	12	13	13	6	11	12	14	0	5	1	87
Global Cash Flow Concepts & Construction	16	10	75	0	7	10	0	0	0	0	118
Information Technology Conference	43	11	44	3	6	38	2	14	8	4	173
Information Technology Symposium	7	0	3	0	2	5	0	0	0	3	20
Instructor Training School	29	1	0	0	1	16	14	3	0	2	66
International Banking (Self-study)	7	0	29	0	0	20	0	0	0	0	56
International Banking School	16	4	18	0	0	3	0	0	1	0	42
Payments Systems Risk Conference	19	10	40	5	8	21	4	0	2	4	113
Real Estate Appraisal Review Online	3	0	32	0	11	0	0	2	0	0	48
Real Estate Appraisal Review School	22	30	48	0	2	16	1	1	1	0	121
Structured Finance: Investment Analysis & Risk Management	23	4	40	5	8	9	0	1	18	0	108
Supervisory Updates & Emerging Issues for Community Financial Institutions	54	23	159	35	18	58	1	2	1	2	353
Supervisory Updates & Emerging Issues for Large, Complex Financial Institutions	31	13	139	4	8	7	12	7	12	0	233
Testifying School	2	1	16	0	2	7	0	0	0	0	28
Grand Total	657	266	1,643	211	253	509	185	55	71	53	3,903
Percentage	16.83	6.82	42.10	5.41	6.48	13.04	4.74	1.41	1.82	1.36	100
Combined Agency and Sponsored Percentage	23.65	NA	47.50	NA	6.48	13.04	4.74	1.41	1.82	1.36	100

session is similar to the development of a conference and is administered and supported by EEO staff.

The Basic International Banking Self-Study was updated and distributed to the agencies on December 23, 2013.

The task force approved a new seminar to the curriculum to be offered in 2014—Agricultural Lending Seminar. One session will be held in Arlington, Virginia, and two regional sessions will be held—one in Kansas City, Missouri, and one in Dallas, Texas. The task force also approved a regional session of the Commercial Real Estate Analysis School to be held in San Francisco, California, in October of 2014.

The task force approves the development and maintenance of the InfoBase product. The FFIEC InfoBase is an online resource that facilitates prompt delivery of introductory, reference, and educational training materials on topics of interest to examination staff from the FFIEC member agencies. The InfoBase content is created and updated by members of the Task Force on Supervision's IT Subcommittee and the Bank Secrecy Act/Anti-Money Laundering (BSA/AML) Working Group.

In 2013, the EEO staff, in conjunction with the IT Subcommittee, continued to coordinate revisions to the IT Examination Handbook InfoBase. Additionally, the EEO staff, in conjunction with the BSA/AML Working Group, continued to update the BSA/AML Examination Manual InfoBase.

Facilities

The FFIEC rents office space, classrooms, and lodging facilities at the FDIC's L. William Seidman Center

in Arlington, Virginia. This facility offers convenient access to two auditoriums and numerous classrooms.

Course Catalogue and Schedule

The course catalogue and schedule are available online at www.ffiec.gov/exam/education.htm.

To obtain a copy, contact:

Karen K. Smith, Manager
FFIEC Examiner Education Office
3501 Fairfax Drive
Room B-3030
Arlington, VA 22226-3550

Phone: (703) 516-5588

Task Force on Information Sharing

The Task Force on Information Sharing promotes and facilitates the sharing (collection, exchange, and access) of electronic information among the Council members in support of the supervision,

regulation, and deposit insurance responsibilities of financial institution regulators. The task force provides a forum for Council members to discuss and address issues affecting the quality, consistency, efficiency, and security of interagency information sharing. Significant matters are referred, with recommendations, to the Council for action, and the task force has delegated authority from the Council to take certain actions.

To the extent possible, the members build on each other's information databases to minimize duplication of effort and promote consistency. In accordance with each member's policy, the members participate in a program to share electronic versions of their examination and inspection reports, and other communications with financial institutions. The members also provide each other with access to their organizations' structures, as well as financial and supervisory information on their regulated entities. The task force and its working groups use a collaborative web-

Task Force on Information Sharing.

site to share information among the Council members. The task force maintains a "Data Exchange Summary" listing the data files exchanged among the Council members and a repository of communications and documents critical to information sharing.

The task force has three working groups to address technology development issues, to perform interagency reconciliation of financial institution structure data, and to develop interagency identity management. In addition, the task force receives demonstrations and reports on agency, financial industry, and other Council initiatives pertaining to technology development (including the production and development status of the interagency Central Data Repository).

Initiatives Addressed in 2013

Technology Issues

The mission of the task force is to identify and implement technologies to make the sharing of interagency data more efficient and to accommodate changes in agency databases and technologies. The task force's Technology Working Group (TWG) meets monthly to develop technological solutions that enhance data sharing and to coordinate the automated transfer of data files between the members. The group tracks weekly developments to provide timely resolutions of data exchange issues.

The TWG continues to develop necessary links and processes to exchange electronic documents, develop an inventory of future technology projects, and upload information to the collaborative website where documents and critical materials pertaining to interagency information exchanges are stored.

Structure Data Reconciliation

The task force's Structure Data Reconciliation Working Group (SDRWG) continued to reconcile structure data about financial institutions regulated by the Council members to ensure that the information reported is consistent and accurate. The SDRWG's quarterly reconcilements have greatly resolved structure data discrepancies among the members.

Identity Management

The Identity Management Working Group continued its efforts to begin developing an Identity Management technology framework among the Council members. These continuing efforts are based on a 2010 white paper developed and presented to the members' Chief Information Officers. This document discussed the new information challenges presented by the recent financial reforms and sought a consensus on the scope and urgency of the efforts needed to meet these challenges going forward. Members are planning a technological solution that establishes a trust arrangement for direct secure electronic access of interagency applications over the Internet. Members will be able to reduce the time and cost of managing security access by other member agencies.

Interagency Loan Data Report

In 2012, the task force created an interagency working group to review and enhance the Interagency Loan Data Report (ILDR), pursuant to a Conference of State Bank Supervisors inquiry in April 2011. The ILDR guidance from 2002 lists 82 possible fields in the ILDR. Of those, five fields were required to be provided with an ILDR submission. The ILDR Working Group recognized that the highest supervisory

value could be achieved by receiving data more consistently in the ILDR. In March 2013, member organizations communicated to banks an increase in the number of required loan data fields from five to 30 to improve efficiency in the data submission process.

Coordination with Other Interagency Information Sharing Entities

The task force continued to coordinate with interagency information sharing entities including the Financial Stability Oversight Council (FSOC) and the Office of Financial Research. These coordination efforts enable the task force to keep apprised of new and emerging issues and to monitor progress on initiatives such as the Global Legal Entity Identifier initiative.

Collaboration Tools

The Collaboration Tools Working Group was created in July 2013 in order to evaluate and make recommendations regarding the FFIEC's use of collaboration tools.

Task Force on Reports

The law establishing the Council and defining its functions requires the Council to develop uniform reporting systems for federally supervised financial institutions and their holding companies and subsidiaries. To meet this objective, the Council established the Task Force on Reports. The task force helps to develop interagency uniformity in the reporting of periodic information that is needed for effective supervision and other public policy purposes. As a consequence, the task force is concerned with issues such as the review and implementation of proposed revisions to reporting requirements; the development and interpretation of reporting

Task Force on Reports meeting.

instructions, including responding to inquiries about the instructions from reporting institutions and the public; the application of accounting standards to specific transactions; the development and application of processing standards; the monitoring of data quality; and the assessment of reporting burden. In addition, the task force works with other organizations, including the Securities and Exchange Commission, the Financial Accounting Standards Board, and the American Institute of Certified Public Accountants. The task force is also responsible for any special projects related to these subjects that the Council may assign.

To help the task force carry out its responsibilities, working groups are organized as needed to handle specialized or technical accounting, reporting, instructional, and processing matters. In this regard, the task force has established a Central Data Repository (CDR) Steering Committee to make business decisions needed to ensure the continued success of the CDR system, monitor its ongoing performance, and report on its status. The CDR is a secure, shared database for collecting, managing, validating,

and distributing data reported in the quarterly Consolidated Reports of Condition and Income (Call Reports) filed by insured banks and savings associations. The CDR also processes and distributes the Uniform Bank Performance Report under the oversight of the Task Force on Surveillance Systems.

Initiatives Addressed in 2013

New Call Report Schedule Implemented in March 2013

After receiving approval under the Paperwork Reduction Act (PRA) from the U.S. Office of Management and Budget (OMB), the FDIC, the FRB, and the OCC (collectively, the banking agencies) implemented new Call Report Schedule RI-C in March 2013 for the collection of disaggregated data on the allowance for loan and lease losses. The schedule is applicable only to institutions with $1 billion or more in total assets. Each such institution discloses, by portfolio category, the quarter-end balance in the allowance disaggregated on the basis of the institution's impairment method and the related recorded investment in loans.

Call Report Revisions Proposed in February 2013

During 2012, the task force evaluated several staff recommendations from the banking agencies and the CFPB for potential Call Report revisions to be implemented in 2013. In late 2012, the task force agreed to request public comment on a number of these revisions. The proposed Call Report changes, for which an initial PRA *Federal Register* notice was published in February 2013, included a question asking whether the reporting institution offers consumer deposit accounts; new items for the balances of consumer transaction and nontransaction savings deposit accounts, the income from three types of service charges on consumer deposit accounts, information about and data on international remittance transfers, trade names used on physical branches and Internet websites that differ from an institution's legal title, and the total liabilities of an institution's parent depository institution holding company that is not a bank or savings and loan holding company; and a clarifying revision to the scope of an item in the changes in equity capital schedule. The proposal also contained new and revised items for collecting data used in the FDIC's deposit insurance pricing model for large and highly complex institutions and related instructional revisions to implement the October 2012 amendments to certain definitions in the FDIC's assessment regulations, supplemented by a tabular presentation of two-year default probabilities by type of consumer loan. As proposed, the collection of consumer deposit account balances and deposit insurance pricing model data would apply to institutions with $1 billion or more and $10 billion or more in total assets, respectively.

The comment period for the proposed Call Report changes closed in April 2013. After considering the comments received, the task force decided to proceed with only two of the revisions as of their proposed June 30, 2013, effective date while continuing to evaluate the remaining proposed changes in light of the comments. The task force made certain modifications to the proposed assessment data items in response to comments on these changes. In June 2013, the OMB approved the revised equity capital reconciliation item and the reporting of the additional assessment data items by large and highly complex institutions. In addition, the Council advised banks and savings associations in June 2013 that any new Call Report requirements resulting from the other revisions proposed in February 2013 would take effect no earlier than December 31, 2013, or March 31, 2014, depending on the change.

In late 2013, the task force concluded its deliberations on the reporting changes remaining from the February 2013 proposal. The Council then approved Call Report revisions that incorporated modifications to the original proposal in response to comments received, including concerns about reporting burden. Effective March 31, 2014, institutions would begin to report trade names used by physical offices and addresses of Internet websites at which deposits are accepted or solicited. All institutions would indicate whether they offer any deposit account products (other than time deposits) primarily intended for consumers, and those institutions with $1 billion or more in total assets that offer such products would report the total balances of their consumer deposit account products. Institutions would provide information about international remittance trans-

fer activity initially as of March 31, 2014, but only semiannually thereafter as of each June 30 and December 31, with the amount of information reported dependent on the number of an institution's transactions per calendar year. Effective March 31, 2015, institutions with $1 billion or more in total assets that offer consumer deposit account products would begin to report three categories of service charge income earned on these products. The proposed item for the total liabilities of certain parent holding companies is not being implemented.

The Council notified reporting institutions about these Call Report revisions, and the banking agencies published a final PRA *Federal Register* notice for these reporting changes in January 2014. Approval of these Call Report changes by the OMB is pending.

Proposed Regulatory Capital Reporting Changes

During the first half of 2013, banking agency regulatory capital experts continued the work that began in 2012 under the auspices of the task force on the development of proposed regulatory capital reporting changes. These changes would align the regulatory capital schedule in the Call Report and, for advanced approaches institutions only, the Advanced Capital Adequacy Framework Regulatory Reporting Requirements (FFIEC 101 report) with the revised regulatory capital rules then being finalized by the banking agencies. In general, an advanced approaches institution is an FDIC-insured depository institution or depository institution holding company with consolidated total assets of $250 billion or more or consolidated total on-balance sheet foreign

exposure of $10 billion or more, a subsidiary of such an institution or holding company, or an entity that elects to apply the advanced approaches capital rules.

Upon the banking agencies' approval of the revised regulatory capital rules in July 2013, the task force completed proposed revisions to the regulatory capital components and ratios portion of Call Report Schedule RC-R, Regulatory Capital, and to the Advanced Approaches Regulatory Capital schedule and nine of the risk-weighted assets schedules in the FFIEC 101 report. After the Council approved these proposed regulatory capital reporting changes, the banking agencies published an initial PRA *Federal Register* notice requesting comment on the proposal in August 2013.

The revised regulatory capital rules apply to advanced approaches institutions beginning January 1, 2014, and to all other institutions beginning January 1, 2015. Therefore, the regulatory capital reporting changes are to be implemented in accordance with this timeline. The revisions to the FFIEC 101 report and the revised regulatory capital components and ratios portion of Call Report Schedule RC-R would take effect for advanced approaches institutions as of March 31, 2014. All other institutions would continue to complete the existing regulatory capital components and ratios portion of Schedule RC-R during 2014 and would then migrate to the revised version of this portion of Schedule RC-R effective March 31, 2015.

After the comment period for the proposed regulatory capital reporting changes ended in October 2013, banking agency regulatory capital experts addressed the comments received, which primarily requested clarification on the applicability and effective dates of the proposed reporting requirements and additional instructional guidance for certain items in the reports. These agency staff members and the task force made appropriate changes to the versions of the revised regulatory capital components and ratios portion of Call Report Schedule RC-R and the revised FFIEC 101 report that had been proposed in August 2013. The Council approved the regulatory capital reporting changes in final form in December 2013. The banking agencies published a final PRA *Federal Register* notice for these reporting changes, and the Council advised reporting institutions about the outcome of the proposal in January 2014. Approval of these changes to Call Report Schedule RC-R and the FFIEC 101 report by the OMB is pending.

Banking agency regulatory capital experts and the task force are nearing completion of a proposal to implement a revised version of the risk-weighted assets portion of Call Report Schedule RC-R in March 2015 that would incorporate the standardized approach for calculating risk-weighted assets under the revised regulatory capital rules. The task force anticipates Council approval of this proposal in the first quarter of 2014 after which the banking agencies would publish an initial PRA *Federal Register* notice requesting comment on the proposed revisions to the reporting of risk-weighted assets in the Call Report.

Central Data Repository

With the existing CDR contract set to expire on November 30, 2013, the CDR Steering Committee focused during early 2013 on preparing for the award of a new contract for hosting, maintaining, and enhancing the CDR. The Technical Evaluation Panel created by the Steering Committee, which was composed of representatives from the FDIC, the FRB, and the OCC, evaluated vendor proposals during the first quarter and determined that the proposal submitted by the incumbent vendor, Unisys, provided the best value to the banking agencies. The Basic Ordering Agreement with Unisys, which was signed on May 15, 2013, has a $40 million ceiling and provides for future task orders for hosting, maintaining, and enhancing the CDR over a six-year period with one two-year option period available.

During 2013, an Innovation Working Group (IWG), which includes CDR Steering Committee members and Unisys representatives, began meeting to identify ways to leverage the CDR for mission effectiveness and to adapt to potential changes in business trends as well as regulatory and technology issues that could affect the CDR and its end users. The IWG meets quarterly to discuss relevant topics which may be significant in determining the CDR roadmap.

Country Exposure Reporting

In late 2012, banking agency international banking experts, under the auspices of the task force, completed a proposal to significantly revise the Country Exposure Report (FFIEC 009 report) and the related publicly available Country Exposure Information Report (FFIEC 009a report). The proposed reporting changes would address the insufficient level of detail in the existing reports about the risks arising from U.S. institutions' foreign exposures. After the Council approved the proposal, the banking agencies published an initial PRA *Federal Register* notice requesting comment on the proposed revisions to the country exposure reporting requirements in January 2013. In broad terms, the proposed revisions to the FFIEC 009 report would increase the number of counterparty categories, add information on the type of claims being reported, provide detail on a limited number of risk mitigants, add more detailed reporting of credit derivatives, add the United States as a country for which exposures are reported, and expand the reporting panel to include savings and loan holding companies. The FFIEC 009a report would be expanded to include additional information for those individual countries for which the disclosure threshold is triggered.

During the second quarter of 2013, banking agency international banking experts considered the comments received on the proposed revisions to the FFIEC 009 and FFIEC 009a reports and, in coordination with the task force, altered certain aspects of the proposed reporting requirements and clarified the draft instructions in response to the comments. The Council approved the final form of the revised country exposure reporting requirements, and the banking agencies published a final PRA notice in the *Federal Register* in June 2013. Based on input from reporting institutions, the task force and the banking agencies agreed that the effective date for the country exposure reporting changes would be December 31, 2013, for current respondents and March 31, 2014, for savings and loan holding companies. The OMB approved these reporting changes in August 2013.

Other Activities

In June 2012, the banking agencies adopted a joint final rule revising their market risk capital rules effective January 1, 2013. The task force revised the Call

Report Schedule RC-R instructions affected by the revised rules in the first quarter of 2013 and eliminated an outdated item from the schedule. During 2013, banking agency market risk capital experts continued their efforts to develop a proposed market risk report (FFIEC 102) for institutions subject to the market risk capital rules. A proposed report is expected to be issued for comment in 2014, with implementation targeted for March 2015.

In November 2012, the task force reported to the Council principals on the results of a statutorily mandated review of the data collected in the Call Report. The statute requires the banking agencies to reduce or eliminate the continued collection of information that they determine is "no longer necessary or appropriate" based on the review of the Call Report. In 2013, the task force began to consider the information obtained from the review to determine where possible burden-reducing revisions to the Call Report may be made. The task force expects to continue these efforts in 2014.

The task force continued to conduct monthly interagency conference calls during 2013 to discuss instructional matters pertaining to FFIEC reports and related accounting issues to reach uniform interagency positions on these issues.

Task Force on Supervision

The Task Force on Supervision (TFOS) coordinates and oversees matters relating to safety-and-soundness supervision and examination of depository institutions. It provides a forum for Council members to promote quality, consistency, and effectiveness in examination and other supervisory practices. While significant issues are referred, with recom-

Task Force on Supervision.

mendations, to the Council for action, the Council has delegated to the task force the authority to make certain decisions and recommendations, provided no task force members disagree. Meetings are held regularly to address and resolve common supervisory issues. The TFOS also maintains supervisory communication protocols to be used in emergencies. These protocols, established by the TFOS, are periodically tested through exercises with task force members and key supervisory personnel.

The TFOS has one subcommittee and two permanent working groups:

- The Information Technology (IT) Subcommittee serves as a forum to address information systems and technology policy issues as they relate to financial institutions and their technology service providers (TSPs). The IT Subcommittee develops and maintains the FFIEC Information Technology Examination Handbook, which consists of a series of topical booklets addressing issues such as information security. This resource is available through an Info-Base on the FFIEC Website. In conjunction with the Task Force on Examiner Education, the IT Subcommittee sponsors an annual FFIEC Information Technology Conference for examiners and periodically holds symposia on emerging information technology and related risks. The IT Subcommittee specifically coordinates with the TFOS's Cybersecurity and Critical Infrastructure Working Group.

- The Bank Secrecy Act/Anti-

Money Laundering (BSA/AML) Working Group seeks to enhance coordination of BSA/AML training, guidance, and policy. Working group coordination includes ongoing communication among federal and state banking agencies and the Financial Crimes Enforcement Network (or FinCEN). The BSA/AML Working Group also meets periodically with other federal agencies, as appropriate. The BSA/AML Working Group builds on existing practices and works to strengthen the activities that are already being pursued by other formal and informal interagency groups providing oversight of various BSA/AML matters. BSA/AML training, guidance, and policy include: procedures and resource materials for examination purposes, joint examiner training related to the FFIEC BSA/AML Examination Manual, outreach to the banking industry on BSA/AML policy matters, and other issues related to consistency of BSA/AML supervision.

- The Cybersecurity and Critical Infrastructure Working Group (CCIWG) was formed in June 2013, in response to the increasing sophistication and volume of cyber threats that pose significant risks to banks of all sizes. The CCIWG promotes coordination across the FFIEC member agencies on cybersecurity and critical infrastructure issues. The group provides a forum for addressing policy issues relating to cybersecurity and critical infrastructure security and the resilience of financial institutions and technology service providers. Working group coordination includes ongoing communications with the intelligence community, law enforcement, and homeland

security agencies. The CCIWG serves as a forum to build on existing efforts to support and strengthen the activities of other interagency and private sector groups that promote financial services sector cybersecurity and critical infrastructure security and resilience. The working group's activities include information sharing, enhancing financial institutions' awareness of risk issues, and examiner training. The CCIWG specifically coordinates with the TFOS's IT Subcommittee.

The task force also establishes working groups to handle individual projects and assignments, as needed.

Initiatives Addressed in 2013

Information Technology

On October 7, 2013, the FFIEC issued a joint statement alerting financial institutions that the discontinuation of support (also known as end of life) for the Microsoft Windows XP operating system (XP) could present operational risks to financial institutions, to TSPs, and to activities supported by other third parties. Effective April 8, 2014, Microsoft will no longer market, support, or provide regular security patches for XP. The FFIEC member agencies expect financial institutions and their TSPs to identify, assess, and manage these risks to ensure that safety and soundness, and the ability to deliver products and services, are not compromised. Financial institutions and TSPs that use XP should follow their risk management processes to address the risk from continued use of XP, consistent with risk management guidance contained in the FFIEC Information Technology Examination Handbook (IT Handbook). The joint statement

addresses some key considerations that institutions should address.

In September 2013, the IT Subcommittee sponsored its annual FFIEC IT Conference for examiners, which highlights current and emerging technology issues affecting insured institutions and their service providers. The conference included a presentation on the IT Subcommittee's review of the supervisory "lessons learned" from the impact of Hurricane Sandy (popularly known as Superstorm Sandy) on the TSPs that the federal banking agencies supervise. In addition, the IT Subcommittee sponsored an FFIEC IT Symposium on the Business Resilience of Technology Service Providers in October 2013. The IT Subcommittee also plans to make revisions, as needed, to appropriate booklets of the IT Handbook. In March 2013, a new feature was added to the IT Handbook InfoBase. (The FFIEC InfoBase is an online resource that facilitates prompt delivery of introductory, reference, and educational training materials on topics of interest to examination staff from the FFIEC member agencies.) The new feature provides bankers, agency personnel, and other interested parties with the ability to register and receive notifications of additions, changes, and deletions to the InfoBase. The agencies added these enhanced user delivery options to ensure timely communication of material changes to the InfoBase.

Interagency Uniform Agreement on the Classification of Assets

In October 2013, the federal banking agencies jointly issued the Uniform Agreement on the Classification and Appraisal of Securities Held by Depository Institutions. This issuance culminated the work of a TFOS-sponsored, interagency working group assigned to update the 2004 Uniform Agreement on the Classification of Assets and Appraisal of Securities Held by Banks and Thrifts. The recently issued statement reiterates the importance of financial institutions having a robust investment analysis process and the agencies' longstanding asset classification definitions. It also addressed the requirements of Section 939A of the Dodd-Frank Act, which directed the agencies to remove any reference to credit ratings published by a nationally recognized statistical rating organization (or NRSRO) and replace them with appropriate standards of creditworthiness. The guidance provides examples to demonstrate the appropriate application of the new standards of creditworthiness consistent with the agencies' longstanding asset classification definitions.

Proposed Supplemental Guidance on Income Tax Allocation Agreements

In December 2013, the federal banking agencies issued for public comment a Proposed Addendum to the Interagency Policy Statement on Income Tax Allocation in a Holding Company Structure. The proposed supplemental guidance addresses income tax allocation agreements involving holding companies and insured depository institutions. It clarifies how sections 23A and 23B of the Federal Reserve Act, which establish certain restrictions on and requirements for transactions between depository institutions and affiliates, apply to tax allocation agreements.

BSA/AML

During 2013, the BSA/AML Working Group continued its work to update the BSA/AML Examination Manual. Also during September 2013, the working group sponsored its seventh FFIEC Advanced

BSA/AML Specialists Conference. Overall, feedback from the conference was positive. The agencies also continued to share information with other agency partners in monitoring and enforcing BSA/AML requirements and standards.

Corrective Program Comparative Review

During 2013, the task force formed a working group to review and share information relative to corrective action processes of the banking agencies (FDIC, FRB, and OCC). The review was conducted, in part, to address recommendations from the Government Accountability Office and the agencies' respective Offices of Inspector General relative to the Prompt Corrective Action (or PCA) framework, the promptness of regulatory actions, and differences in the types of safety and soundness-related enforcement actions implemented by the agencies. Each agency discussed practices which it found to be effective in implementing that agency's enforcement action program. The review concluded that the agencies have a wide breadth of enforcement action tools, both formal and informal, that can be effective in obtaining corrective action at their respective supervised institutions.

Task Force on Surveillance Systems

The Task Force on Surveillance Systems oversees the development and implementation of uniform interagency surveillance and monitoring systems. It provides a forum for the members to discuss best practices to be used in those systems and to consider the development of new financial analysis tools. The task force's principal

objective has been to develop and produce the Uniform Bank Performance Report (UBPR). UBPRs present financial data of individual financial institutions and peer group statistics for current and historical periods. These reports are important tools for completing supervisory evaluations of a financial institution's condition and performance, as well as for planning onsite examinations. The federal and state banking agencies also use the data from these reports in their automated monitoring systems to identify potential or emerging risks in insured financial institutions.

A UBPR is produced for each insured bank and savings association in the United States that is supervised by the FRB, FDIC, or OCC. UBPR data are also available to all state bank supervisors. While the UBPR is principally designed to meet the examination and surveillance needs of the federal and state banking agencies, the task force also makes the UBPR available to financial institutions and the public through a public website, www.ffiec.gov/ UBPR.htm.

Initiatives Addressed in 2013

Content Working Group

The task force established the Content Working Group to perform a complete review of the UBPR (excluding the fiduciary data activities and liquidity pages that were reviewed in 2010 and 2011) and make recommendations for potential enhancements.

Technology Working Group

The task force established the Technology Working Group to look at ways to improve the usability of the UBPR. For example, the development of various presentation options (i.e., graphs, charts) and the creation of a mobile application will be explored.

Supplementary Analysis Working Group

The task force established the Supplementary Analysis Working Group to identify other analytics (besides the UBPR) that could be developed and maintained under the purview of the task force.

Review of the Online and PDF UBPR User's Guide

The new online UBPR User's Guide and related PDF UBPR User's Guide are based on the existing CDR system taxonomy. Because the taxonomy is very extensive, consisting of thousands of UBPR and Call Report concepts, the task force reviewed the taxonomy to ensure the accuracy and consistency of all UBPR concepts (which includes descriptions, narratives, and formulas) contained in both the online and PDF UBPR User's Guide. Changes were made resulting in improved accuracy and consistency of UBPR concepts.

UBPR Production and Delivery

During 2013, UBPRs for December 31, 2012; March 31, 2013; June 30, 2013; and September 30, 2013, were produced and delivered to federal and state banking agencies. Additionally, the UBPR section of the FFIEC Website was utilized to deliver the same data to financial institutions and the general public. The task force strives to deliver the most up-to-date UBPR data to all users. Thus, the data for the current quarter is updated nightly and the data for previous quarters is updated regularly. Frequent updating allows

the UBPR to remain synchronized with new Call Report data as it is being submitted by financial institutions.

Other Activities

The Technology Working Group is exploring the possibility of creating a bank financial data application (APP) that could be used on either a mobile device or a desktop computer. The APP is envisioned as a new analytical tool that will use data from a variety of sources (including the UBPR and Call Report) to better assess the risk of a particular financial institution.

The Supplementary Analysis Working Group is working with agency personnel to help identify the various analytical tools and datasets currently used at the respective agencies. Once such tools and datasets are identified, the working group will determine whether such tools and datasets could be better shared among the agencies to enhance the UBPR or create a new FFIEC analytical tool.

UBPR Information on the FFIEC Website

UBPR Availability

To provide broad industry and public access to information about the financial condition of insured financial institutions, the task force publishes UBPR data for each institution shortly after the underlying Call Report is filed in the CDR. The UBPR is frequently refreshed to reflect amendments to underlying Call Report data and to incorporate any content-based changes agreed to by the task force. The online UBPR is a dynamic report that is closely synchronized with the underlying Call Report.

Other UBPR Reports

Web-based statistical reports supporting UBPR analysis are available and are updated nightly with the data for the current quarter and regularly for previous quarters. These reports (1) summarize the performance of all UBPR peer groups (determined by size, location, and business line); (2) detail

Task Force on Surveillance Systems meeting.

the distribution of UBPR performance ratios for financial institutions in each of these peer groups; (3) list the individual financial institutions included in each peer group; and (4) compare a financial institution to the performance of a user-defined custom peer group.

Custom Peer Group Tool

The Custom Peer Group Tool allows industry professionals, regulators, and the general public to create custom peer groups based on financial and geographical criteria. The tool can then display all UBPR pages with peer group statistics and percentile rankings derived from the custom peer group. The Custom Peer Group Tool can re-compute the entire UBPR using a custom peer group of up to 2,000 financial institutions and deliver the results usually within seconds.

Bulk Data Download

The UBPR database within the CDR, which contains all data appearing on report pages for all financial institutions, may be downloaded as either a delimited file or in XBRL format. The service is free, and downloads are typically fast.

Additional information about the UBPR, including status, descriptions of changes, and the UBPR Users Guide, is found at www.ffiec.gov/UBPR.htm. The site also provides access to the reports described above. For questions about the UBPR, contact support by calling 1-888-237-3111, e-mailing cdr.help@ffiec.gov, or writing the Council at:

FFIEC
3501 Fairfax Drive, Room B7081a
Arlington, VA 22226-3550

THE FEDERAL FINANCIAL INSTITUTION REGULATORY AGENCIES AND THEIR SUPERVISED INSTITUTIONS

The FRB, FDIC, OCC, and NCUA have primary federal supervisory jurisdiction over 13,649 domestically chartered banks, savings associations, and federally insured credit unions. On December 31, 2013, these financial institutions held total assets of approximately $18.2 trillion. The FRB has primary federal supervisory responsibility for commercial bank holding companies (BHCs) and for savings and loan holding companies (SLHCs).

Three banking agencies on the Council have authority to oversee the operations of U.S. branches and agencies of foreign banks. The International Banking Act of 1978 (IBA) authorizes the OCC to license federal branches and agencies of foreign banks and permits U.S. branches that accept only wholesale deposits to apply for insurance with the FDIC. According to the Federal Deposit Insurance Corporation Improvement Act of 1991 (FDICIA), foreign banks that wish to operate insured entities in the United States and accept retail deposits must organize under separate U.S. charters. Existing insured retail branches may continue to operate as branches. The IBA also subjects those U.S. offices of foreign banks to many provisions of the Federal Reserve Act and the Bank Holding Company Act. The IBA gives primary examining authority to the OCC, FDIC, and various state authorities for the offices within their jurisdictions. The IBA also gives the FRB residual examining authority over all U.S. banking operations of foreign banks.

The Dodd-Frank Act provides statutory authority to the CFPB to conduct examinations of insured depository entities with total assets over $10 billion and their affiliates (in addition to certain nonbank entities) to ensure consumer financial products and services conform to certain federal consumer financial laws.

Board of Governors of the Federal Reserve System

The Federal Reserve Board (FRB) was established in 1913. It is headed by a seven-member Board of Governors; each member is appointed by the President, with the advice and consent of the Senate, for a 14-year term. Subject to confirmation by the Senate, the President selects one Board member to serve a four-year term as Chairperson and two members to serve as Vice Chairs; one serves in the absence of the Chairperson and the other is designated as Vice Chair for Supervision. The Chairperson also serves as a voting member of the Financial Stability Oversight Council (FSOC). One member of the Board of Governors serves as the Board's representative to the FFIEC. The FRB's activities most relevant to the work of the Council are the following:

- overseeing the quality and efficiency of the examination and supervision function of the 12 Federal Reserve Banks;

- developing, issuing, implementing, and communicating regulations, supervisory policies, and guidance, and taking appropriate enforcement actions applicable to those organizations that are within the FRB's supervisory oversight authority;

- approving or denying applications for mergers, acquisitions, and changes in control by state member banks, SLHCs, and BHCs (including financial holding companies (FHCs)); applications for foreign operations of member banks and Edge Act and agreement corporations; and applications by foreign banks to establish or acquire U.S. banks and to establish U.S. branches, agencies, or representative offices; and

- supervising and regulating:

  - State member banks (i.e., state-chartered banks that are members of the Federal Reserve System);

  - BHCs, including FHCs;

  - SLHCs;[1]

  - Edge Act and agreement corporations; select non-bank financial firms;

  - International operations of banking organizations headquartered in the United States and the domestic activities of foreign banking organizations, in conjunction with the responsible licensing authorities; as well as,

  - Nonbank financial firms designated as systemically important by FSOC.

Other supervisory and regulatory responsibilities of the FRB include monitoring compliance by entities under the Board's jurisdiction with other statutes (e.g., the anti-money laundering provisions of the Bank Secrecy Act), monitoring compliance with certain statutes that protect consumers in credit and deposit transactions, regulating margin requirements on securities transactions, and regulating transactions between banking affiliates.

Policy decisions are implemented

---

1. The FRB's role as supervisor of BHCs, FHCs, and SLHCs is to review and assess the consolidated organization's operations, risk-management systems, and capital adequacy to ensure that the holding company and its nonbank subsidiaries do not threaten the viability of the company's depository institutions. In this role, the FRB serves as the "umbrella supervisor" of the consolidated organization. In fulfilling this role, the FRB relies, to the fullest extent possible, on information and analysis provided by the appropriate supervisory authority of the company's depository institutions, securities, or insurance subsidiaries.

by the FRB or under delegated authority to the Director for the Division of Banking Supervision and Regulation, the Director of the Division of Consumer and Community Affairs, and to the 12 Federal Reserve Banks—each of which has operational responsibility within a specific geographical area. The Reserve Bank Districts are headquartered in Boston, New York, Philadelphia, Cleveland, Richmond, Atlanta, Chicago, St. Louis, Minneapolis, Kansas City, Dallas, and San Francisco. Each Reserve Bank has a president (chief executive officer) who serves for five years and is appointed by the Reserve Bank's class B and class C directors, and other executive officers who report directly to the president. Among other responsibilities, a Reserve Bank employs a staff of examiners who examine state member banks and Edge Act and agreement corporations, conduct SLHC/BHC inspections, and examine the international operations of foreign banks—whose head offices are usually located within the Reserve Bank's District. When appropriate, examiners also visit the overseas offices of U.S. banking organizations to obtain financial and operating information to evaluate adherence to safe and sound banking practices.

National banks, which must be members of the Federal Reserve System, are chartered, regulated, and supervised by the OCC. State-chartered banks may apply to and be accepted for membership in the Federal Reserve System, after which they are subject to the supervision and regulation of the FRB, which is coordinated with the state's banking authority. Insured state-chartered banks that are not members of the Federal Reserve System are regulated and supervised by the FDIC. The FRB also has overall responsibility for the supervision of foreign banking operations, including both U.S. banks operating abroad and foreign banks operating branches within the United States.

The Dodd-Frank Act directs the FRB to collect assessments, fees, and other charges that are equal to the expenses incurred by the Federal Reserve to carry out its responsibilities with respect to supervision of (1) BHCs and SLHCs with assets equal to or greater than $50 billion and (2) all nonbank financial companies supervised by the FRB.

Additionally, the Dodd-Frank Act created an independent CFPB within the Federal Reserve System.

The FRB covers the expenses of the CFPB's operations with revenue it generates principally from assessments on the 12 Federal Reserve Banks.

Consumer Financial
Protection Bureau

Consumer Financial Protection Bureau

The Consumer Financial Protection Bureau (CFPB) was created in 2010 by the Dodd-Frank Act and assumed transferred authorities from other federal agencies, and other new authorities, on July 21, 2011. The CFPB is an independent agency and is funded principally by transfers from the FRB up to a limit set forth in the statute. The CFPB requests transfers from the Board in amounts that are reasonably necessary to carry out its mission. Funding is capped at a pre-set percentage of the total 2009 operating expenses of the Federal Reserve System, subject to an annual adjustment. The Director of the CFPB serves on the FDIC Board of Directors and the Financial Stability Oversight Council.

The CFPB seeks to foster a consumer financial marketplace where customers can clearly see prices and risks up front and can easily make product comparisons; in which no one can build a business model around unfair, deceptive, or abusive practices; and that works for American consumers, responsible providers, and the economy as a whole. To accomplish this, the CFPB works to help consumer financial markets operate by making rules more effective, by consistently and fairly enforcing those rules, and by empowering consumers to take more control over their economic lives.

The Dodd-Frank Act sets forth the following functions for the CFPB:

- conducting financial education programs;

- collecting, investigating, and responding to consumer complaints;

- collecting, researching, monitoring, and publishing information relevant to the identification of risks to consumers and the proper functioning of financial markets;

- issuing rules, orders, and guidance implementing federal consumer financial laws;

- taking appropriate enforcement action to address violations of federal consumer financial law; and

- supervising covered entities to assess compliance with federal consumer financial law, obtain information about the activities and compliance systems or procedures of such persons, and detect and assess risks to consumers and markets for consumer financial products and services.

The CFPB has statutory authority to, among other things, conduct examinations of and require reports from entities subject to its supervisory authority. The CFPB has supervisory authority over:

- Insured depository institutions and credit unions with total assets over $10 billion and their affiliates. These institutions collectively hold more than 75 percent of the banking industry's assets.

- Certain nondepository entities regardless of size—mortgage companies (originators, brokers, and servicers, as well as related loan modification or foreclosure relief services firms), payday lenders, and private education lenders. The CFPB can also supervise the larger players, or "larger participants," as defined by rule, in consumer financial markets, and certain nondepository entities that it determines are posing a risk to consumers in connection with the offering or provision of consumer financial products or services. To date, the CFPB has published final rules that allow it to supervise larger participants in the

— consumer reporting market (these entities have more than $7 million in annual receipts resulting from consumer reporting);

— consumer debt collection market (these entities have annual receipts of more than $10 million resulting from consumer debt collection); and

— student loan servicing market, effective March 1, 2014 (these entities have account volume that exceeds one million).

The CFPB's supervisory activities are conducted by the Division of Supervision, Enforcement, Fair Lending and Equal Opportunity. The Division is headquartered in Washington, DC, with regional offices in San Francisco (West), Chicago (Midwest), New York (Northeast), and Washington, DC (Southeast). Examination staff is assigned to each of the four regions.

Federal Deposit Insurance Corporation

Congress created the Federal Deposit Insurance Corporation (FDIC) in 1933 to promote stability and public confidence in our nation's banking system. The FDIC accomplishes its mission by insuring deposits, examining and otherwise supervising financial institutions for safety and soundness and consumer protection, and managing receiverships. In its unique role as deposit insurer, the FDIC works in cooperation with other federal and state regulatory agencies to identify, monitor, and address risks to the Deposit Insurance Fund (DIF) posed by insured depository institutions.

Management of the FDIC is vested in a five-member Board of Directors. No more than three board members may be of the same political party. Three of the directors are appointed by the President, with the advice and consent of the Senate, for six-year terms. One of the three appointed directors is designated by the President as Chairman for a five-year term and another is designated as Vice Chairman. The other two board members are the Comptroller of the Currency and the Director of the Consumer Financial Protection Bureau. The Chairman also serves as a member of the Financial Stability Oversight Council.

Operational Structure

The FDIC's operations are organized into three major program areas: insurance, supervision, and receivership management. A description of each of these areas follows:

Insurance: The FDIC maintains stability and public confidence in the U.S. financial system by providing deposit insurance. As insurer, the

FDIC must continually monitor changes in the economy, financial markets, and banking system and evaluate and manage the effect of these changes on the adequacy of the DIF. When an insured depository institution fails, the FDIC ensures that the financial institution's customers have timely access to their insured deposits and other services.

The FDIC, through its Division of Insurance and Research, provides the public with a sound deposit insurance system by publishing comprehensive statistical information on banking; identifying and analyzing emerging risks; conducting research that supports deposit insurance, banking policy, and risk assessment; assessing the adequacy of the DIF; and maintaining a risk-based premium system.

The Dodd-Frank Act revised the statutory authorities governing the FDIC's management of the DIF. As a result, the FDIC has developed a comprehensive, long-term management plan for the DIF to reduce pro-cyclicality in the deposit insurance system and maintain a positive fund balance even during a banking crisis. The plan sets an appropriate target fund size and a strategy for setting assessment rates and dividends. The FDIC has also adopted a Restoration Plan to ensure that the reserve ratio reaches the statutorily mandated level of 1.35 percent by September 30, 2020, as required by the Dodd-Frank Act.

Supervision: The FDIC has primary federal supervisory authority over insured state-chartered banks that are not members of the Federal Reserve System and for state-chartered savings associations. As deposit insurer, the FDIC also has backup examination and enforcement authority over all insured institutions. Accordingly, the FDIC can examine for insurance purposes any insured financial institution, either independently or in cooperation with state or other federal supervisory authorities. The FDIC can also recommend that the appropriate federal banking agency take action against an insured institution and may do so itself if it deems necessary. The Dodd-Frank Act also authorizes the FDIC to manage the failure of systemically important financial institutions (SIFIs). In exercising this authority, the FDIC monitors risk within and across large, complex financial companies for resolution readiness purposes. The FDIC has maintained and/or introduced various initiatives to support and enhance its systems of control and promote effective supervision of SIFIs.

The FDIC's supervisory activities for risk management and consumer protection are primarily organized into two divisions: the Division of Risk Management Supervision (RMS) and the Division of Depositor and Consumer Protection (DCP). RMS oversees the safety and soundness of FDIC-supervised institutions and carries out the FDIC's backup examination and enforcement authorities. DCP oversees the FDIC's consumer protection supervisory functions, including its examination and enforcement programs for FDIC-supervised institutions with assets of $10 billion or less. Under the Dodd-Frank Act, the FDIC also retains examination and supervisory authority for several laws and regulations, including the Community Reinvestment Act, without regard to the size of an institution.

RMS and DCP are further organized into six regional offices located in Atlanta, Chicago, Dallas, Kansas City, New York, and San Francisco. There are two area offices located in Boston (reporting to New York) and Memphis (reporting to Dallas). In addition to the regional and area offices, the FDIC maintains 86 field offices for risk management and 76 field offices for compliance. Dedicated examiners are assigned to the largest financial institutions.

Receivership Management: Bank resolutions are handled by the FDIC's Division of Resolutions and Receiverships (DRR). In protecting insured depositors, the FDIC is statutorily charged with resolving failed depository institutions at the least possible cost to the DIF. In carrying out this responsibility, the FDIC engages in several activities, including paying off depositors, arranging the purchase of assets and assumption of liabilities of failed institutions, effecting insured deposit transfers between institutions, and creating and operating temporary bridge banks until a resolution can be accomplished.

DRR maintains personnel in its field office in Dallas and its temporary satellite office in Jacksonville, Florida; it also maintains staff in each of the FDIC regional offices.

In addition, the Office of Complex Financial Institutions (OCFI) implements the FDIC's systemic resolution responsibilities under the Dodd-Frank Act, including resolution planning and promoting cross-border cooperation and coordination with respect to an orderly resolution of a globally active SIFI. Prior to the recent crisis, the FDIC's receivership authority was limited to federally insured banks and thrift institutions. No regulator had the authority to place the holding company or affiliates of an insured depository institution, or to place any other non-bank financial company, into an FDIC receivership.

The preferred option for the resolution of a SIFI is for the firm to file for reorganization or liquidation under the U.S. Bankruptcy Code, just as any failed non-financial company would. The Orderly Liquidation Authority gives the FDIC the powers necessary to potentially resolve a failing systemic bank holding company or a systemic financial company in an orderly manner that imposes accountability on shareholders, creditors, and the management of the failed company, while mitigating systemic risk and imposing no cost on taxpayers. This serves as a potential alternative when bankruptcy would have serious adverse effects on U.S. financial stability.

National Credit Union Administration

The National Credit Union Administration (NCUA), established by Congress in 1970 through section 1752a of the Federal Credit Union Act, is the independent federal agency that supervises the nation's federal credit union system. A three-member bipartisan board, appointed by the President for six-year terms, manages the NCUA. The President also selects one board member to serve as the Chairman. The Chairman also serves as a member of the Financial Stability Oversight Council.

The NCUA's main responsibilities are as follows:

- charter, regulate, and supervise more than 4,100 federal credit unions in the United States and its territories;

- administer the National Credit Union Share Insurance Fund (NCUSIF), which insures member share accounts in just over 6,500 federal and state-chartered credit unions;

- administer the Temporary Corporate Credit Union Stabilization Fund, which has borrowing authority from the U.S. Treasury and assessment authority to resolve corporate credit union issues; and

- manage the Central Liquidity Facility, created to improve the financial stability of credit unions by providing liquidity to the credit union system.

The NCUA also has statutory authority to examine and supervise NCUSIF-insured, state-chartered credit unions in coordination with state regulators.

The NCUA is headquartered in Alexandria, Virginia, and has five regional offices across the United States to administer its responsibilities for chartering and supervising credit unions. Additionally, the Asset Management and Assistance Center located in Austin, Texas, manages the recovery of assets for liquidated credit unions. NCUA examiners conduct on-site examinations and supervision of each federal credit union and selected state-chartered credit unions. The NCUA is funded by the credit unions it regulates and insures.

Office of the Comptroller of the Currency

The Office of the Comptroller of the Currency (OCC) is the oldest federal bank regulatory agency, established as a bureau of the Treasury Department by the National Currency Act of 1863. It is headed by the Comptroller of the Currency, who is appointed to a five-year term by the President with the advice and consent of the Senate. The Comptroller is also a Director of the FDIC and a member of the Financial Stability Oversight Council.

The OCC was created by Congress to charter, regulate, and supervise national banks. On July 21, 2011, pursuant to the Dodd-Frank Act, the OCC assumed supervisory responsibility for federal savings associations, as well as rulemaking authority relating to all savings associations. The OCC regulates and supervises 1,245 national banks and trust companies, 515 federal savings associations, and 48 federal branches of foreign banks—accounting for approximately 69 percent of the total assets of all U.S. commercial banks, federal savings associations, and branches of foreign banks. The OCC seeks to ensure that national banks and federal savings associations (collectively "banks") safely and soundly manage their risks, comply with applicable laws, compete effectively with other providers of financial services, offer products and services that meet the needs of customers, and provide fair access to financial services and fair treatment of their customers.

The OCC's mission-critical programs include:

- chartering banks and issuing interpretations related to permissible banking activities;

- establishing and communicating regulations, policies, and operating guidance applicable to banks; and

- supervising the national system of banks and savings associations through on-site examinations, off-site monitoring, systemic risk analyses, and appropriate enforcement activities.

To meet its objectives, the OCC maintains a nationwide staff of bank examiners and other professional and support personnel. Headquartered in Washington, DC, the OCC has four district offices, which are located in Chicago, Dallas, Denver, and New York. In addition, the OCC maintains a network of 73 field offices and 20 satellite locations in cities throughout the United States, as well as resident examiner teams in 24 of the largest national banking companies and an examining office in London, England.

The Comptroller receives advice on policy and operational issues from an Executive Committee comprised of senior agency officials who lead major business units.

The OCC is funded primarily by semiannual assessments on banks, interest revenue from its investment in U.S. Treasury securities, and other fees. The OCC does not receive congressional appropriations for any of its operations.

ASSETS, LIABILITIES, AND NET WORTH of U.S. Commercial Banks, Savings Institutions, and Credit Unions as of December 31, 2013[1]

Billions of dollars

Item	Total	U.S. Commercial Banks[2]			U.S. Branches and Agencies of Foreign Banks[6]	Savings Institutions[4]		Credit Unions[3]	
		National	State Member[5]	State Non-Member		OCC Regulated Federal Charter	FDIC Regulated State Charter[7]	Federal Charter	State Charter
Total assets	*18,193*	*9,445*	*2,060*	*2,172*	*2,402*	*702*	*350*	*571*	*491*
Total loans and receivables (net)	8,992	4,781	952	1,417	565	403	234	341	299
Loans secured by real estate[8]	4,434	2,229	512	860	30	260	204	176	163
Consumer loans[9]	1,653	930	72	247		98	6	166	134
Commercial and industrial loans	1,888	1,038	244	249	291	35	24	3	4
All other loans and lease receivables[10]	1,160	673	138	84	244	17	3	0	1
LESS: Allowance for loan and lease losses	143	89	14	23	–	7	3	4	3
Federal funds sold and securities purchased under agreements to resell	604	381	33	10	177	1	1	0	1
Cash and due from depository institutions[11]	2,821	1,095	379	160	976	57	17	70	67
Securities and other obligations[12]	3,379	1,824	476	423	142	207	72	134	101
U.S. government obligations[13]	716	220	74	91	42	30	57	115	87
Obligations of state and local governments[14]	292	143	52	85		6	6	–	–
Other securities	2,371	1,461	350	247	100	171	9	19	14
Other assets[15]	2,397	1,364	220	162	542	34	26	26	23
Total liabilities	*16,419*	*8,391*	*1,834*	*1,916*	*2,401*	*620*	*308*	*510*	*439*
Total deposits and shares[16]	13,250	7,034	1,648	1,707	1,148	540	262	486	425
Federal funds purchased and securities sold under agreements to repurchase	675	251	49	33	313	18	9	2	0
Other borrowings[17]	1,222	658	68	145	240	49	34	18	10
Other liabilities[18]	1,272	448	69	31	700	13	3	4	4
Net worth[19]	*1,774*	*1,054*	*226*	*256*	*1*	*82*	*42*	*61*	*52*
Memorandum: Number of institutions reporting	13,649	1,212	850	3,871	226	497	439	4,105	2,449

Footnotes to Tables

1. The table covers institutions, including those in Puerto Rico and U.S. territories and possessions, insured by the Federal Deposit Insurance Corporation or National Credit Union Savings Insurance Fund. All branches and agencies of foreign banks in the United States, but excluding any in Puerto Rico and U.S. territories and possessions, are covered whether or not insured. Excludes Edge Act and Agreement corporations that are not subsidiaries of U.S. commercial banks.

2. Reflects fully consolidated statements of FDIC-insured U.S. commercial banks—including their foreign branches, foreign subsidiaries, branches in Puerto Rico and U.S. territories and possessions, and FDIC insured banks in Puerto Rico and U.S. territories and possessions. Excludes bank holding companies.

3. Data are for federally insured natural person credit unions only.

4. Reflects fully consolidated statements of Savings Institutions—including Stock Savings Banks, Mutual Savings Banks, Stock Savings & Loan Associations, and Mutual Savings & Loan Associations that are Federally Chartered or that are State Chartered and not Federal Reserve Members.

5. Includes State Member Savings Banks and State Member Cooperative Banks.

6. These institutions are not required to file reports of income.

7. Includes State Chartered Savings Associations formerly regulated by the Office of Thrift Supervision.

8. Includes loans secured by residential property, commercial property, farm-land (including improvements) and unimproved land; and construction loans secured by real estate.

9. Includes loans, except those secured by real estate, to individuals for household, family, and other personal expenditures including both installment and single payment loans. Net of unearned income on installment loans.

10. Includes loans to financial institutions, for purchasing or carrying securities, to finance agricultural production and other loans to farmers (except those secured by real estate), to states and political subdivisions and public authorities, and miscellaneous types of loans.

Notes continue on the next page

INCOME AND EXPENSES of U.S. Commercial Banks, Savings Institutions, and Credit Unions for the Twelve Months Ending December 31, 2013[1]

Billions of dollars

Item	Total	U.S. Commercial Banks[2]			Savings Institutions[4]		Credit Unions[3]	
		National	State Member[5]	State Non-Member	OCC Regu-lated Federal Charter	FDIC Regu-lated State Charter[7]	Federal Charter	State Charter
Operating income:	774	459	89	117	46	13	27	23
Interest and fees on loans	408	226	39	78	24	10	17	14
Other interest and dividend income	97	65	12	10	4	2	2	2
All other operating income	269	168	38	29	18	1	8	7
Operating expenses:	544	314	63	82	33	10	23	19
Salaries and benefits	205	120	27	29	8	4	9	8
Interest on deposits and shares	37	17	3	8	3	1	3	2
Interest on other borrowed money	20	13	1	3	2	1	0	0
Provision for loan and lease losses	35	19	3	6	4	0	2	1
All other operating expenses	247	145	29	36	16	4	9	8
Net operating income	*230*	*145*	*26*	*35*	*13*	*3*	*4*	*4*
Securities gains and losses	4	3	0	1	0	0	0	0
Extraordinary items	0	0	0	0	0	0	–	–
Income taxes	69	47	7	10	4	1	–	–
Net income	*165*	*101*	*19*	*26*	*9*	*2*	*4*	*4*
Memorandum: Number of institutions reporting	13,423	1,212	850	3,871	497	439	4,105	2,449

11. Includes vault cash, cash items in process of collection, and balances with U.S. and foreign banks and other depository institutions (including demand and time deposits and certificates of deposit for all categories of institutions).

12. Includes government and corporate securities, including mortgage-backed securities and obligations of states and political subdivisions and of U.S. government agencies and corporations.

13. U.S. Treasury securities and securities of, and loans to, U.S. government agencies and corporations.

14. Securities issued by states and political subdivisions and public authorities, except for U.S. branches and agencies of foreign banks that do not report these securities separately. Loans to states and political subdivisions and

public authorities are included in "All other loans and lease receivables."

15. Customers liabilities on acceptances, real property owned, various accrual accounts, and miscellaneous assets. For U.S. branches and agencies of foreign banks, also includes net due from head office and other related institutions.

16. Includes demand, savings, and time deposits, (including certificates of deposit at commercial banks, U.S. branches and agencies of foreign banks, and savings banks), credit balances at U.S. agencies of foreign banks and share balances at credit unions (including certificates of deposit, NOW accounts, and share draft accounts). For U.S. commercial banks, includes deposits in foreign offices, branches in U.S. territories and possessions, and Edge Act and Agreement corporation subsidiaries.

17. Includes interest-bearing demand notes issued to the U.S. Treasury, borrowing from Federal Reserve Banks and Federal Home Loan Banks, subordinated debt, limited life preferred stock, and other nondeposit borrowing.

18. Includes depository institutions own mortgage borrowing, liability for capitalized leases, liability on acceptances executed, various accrual accounts, and miscellaneous liabilities. For U.S. branches and agencies of foreign banks, also includes net owed to head office and other related institutions.

19. Includes capital stock, surplus, capital reserves, and undivided profits.

NOTE: Data are rounded to nearest billion. Consequently some information may not reconcile precisely. Additionally, balances less than $500 million will show as zero.

APPENDIX A: RELEVANT STATUTES

Federal Financial Institutions Examination Council Act

12 U.S.C. § 3301. Declaration of purpose

It is the purpose of this chapter to establish a Financial Institutions Examination Council which shall prescribe uniform principles and standards for the Federal examination of financial institutions by the Office of the Comptroller of the Currency, the Federal Deposit Insurance Corporation, the Board of Governors of the Federal Reserve System, the Federal Home Loan Bank Board, and the National Credit Union Administration and make recommendations to promote uniformity in the supervision of these financial institutions. The Council's actions shall be designed to promote consistency in such examination and to insure progressive and vigilant supervision.

12 U.S.C. § 3302. Definitions

As used in this chapter—

(1) the term "Federal financial institutions regulatory agencies" means the Office of the Comptroller of the Currency, the Board of Governors of the Federal Reserve System, the Federal Deposit Insurance Corporation, the Office of Thrift Supervision, and the National Credit Union Administration;

(2) the term "Council" means the Financial Institutions Examination Council; and

(3) the term "financial institution" means a commercial bank, a savings bank, a trust company, a savings association, a building and loan association, a homestead association, a cooperative bank, or a credit union[.]

12 U.S.C. § 3303. Financial Institutions Examination Council

(a) Establishment; composition

There is established the Financial Institutions Examination Council which shall consist of—

(1) the Comptroller of the Currency,

(2) the Chairman of the Board of Directors of the Federal Deposit Insurance Corporation,

(3) a Governor of the Board of Governors of the Federal Reserve System designated by the Chairman of the Board,

(4) the **Director of the Consumer Financial Protection Bureau,**[1]

(5) the Chairman of the National Credit Union Administration Board; and

(6) the Chairman of the State Liaison Committee.

(b) Chairmanship

The members of the Council shall select the first chairman of the Council. Thereafter the chairmanship shall rotate among the members of the Council.

(c) Term of office

---

1. The Dodd-Frank Wall Street Reform and Consumer Protection Act of 2010 amended several provisions in the relevant statutes, including excerpts contained in this appendix. Changes are shown as bolded and italicized. The amendments relating to the Consumer Financial Protection Bureau became effective on July 21, 2011.

The term of the Chairman of the Council shall be two years.

(d) Designation of officers and employees

The members of the Council may, from time to time, designate other officers or employees of their respective agencies to carry out their duties on the Council.

(e) Compensation and expenses

Each member of the Council shall serve without additional compensation but shall be entitled to reasonable expenses incurred while carrying out his official duties as such a member.

12 U.S.C. § 3304. Costs and expenses of Council

One-fifth of the costs and expenses of the Council, including the salaries of its employees, shall be paid by each of the Federal financial institutions regulatory agencies. Annual assessments for such share shall be levied by the Council based upon its projected budget for the year, and additional assessments may be made during the year if necessary.

12 U.S.C. § 3305. Functions of Council

(a) Establishment of principles and standards

The Council shall establish uniform principles and standards and report forms for the examination of financial institutions which shall be applied by the Federal financial institutions regulatory agencies.

(b) Making recommendations

regarding supervisory matters and adequacy of supervisory tools

(1) The Council shall make recommendations for uniformity in other supervisory matters, such as, but not limited to, classifying loans subject to country risk, identifying financial institutions in need of special supervisory attention, and evaluating the soundness of large loans that are shared by two or more financial institutions. In addition, the Council shall make recommendations regarding the adequacy of supervisory tools for determining the impact of holding company operations on the financial institutions within the holding company and shall consider the ability of supervisory agencies to discover possible fraud or questionable and illegal payments and practices which might occur in the operation of financial institutions or their holding companies.

(2) When a recommendation of the Council is found unacceptable by one or more of the applicable Federal financial institutions regulatory agencies, the agency or agencies shall submit to the Council, within a time period specified by the Council, a written statement of the reasons the recommendation is unacceptable.

(c) Development of uniform reporting system

The Council shall develop uniform reporting systems for federally supervised financial institutions, their holding companies, and non-financial institution subsidiaries of such institutions or holding companies. The authority to develop uniform reporting systems shall not restrict or amend the requirements of section 78l(i) of Title 15.

(d) Conducting schools for examiners and assistant examiners

The Council shall conduct schools for examiners and assistant examiners employed by the Federal financial institutions regulatory agencies. Such schools shall be open to enrollment by employees of State financial institutions supervisory agencies and employees of the Federal Housing Finance Board under conditions specified by the Council.

(e) Affect on Federal regulatory agency research and development of new financial institutions supervisory agencies

Nothing in this chapter shall be construed to limit or discourage Federal regulatory agency research and development of new financial institutions supervisory methods and tools, nor to preclude the field testing of any innovation devised by any Federal regulatory agency.

(f) Annual report

Not later than April 1 of each year, the Council shall prepare an annual report covering its activities during the preceding year.

(g) Flood insurance

The Council shall consult with and assist the Federal entities for lending regulation, as such term is defined in section 4121(a) of Title 42, in developing and coordinating uniform standards and requirements for use by regulated lending institutions under the national flood insurance program.

12 U.S.C. § 3306. State liaison

To encourage the application of uniform examination principles and standards by State and Federal supervisory agencies, the Council shall establish a liaison committee composed of five representatives of State agencies which supervise financial institutions which shall meet at least twice a year with the Council. Members of the liaison committee shall receive a reasonable allowance for necessary expenses incurred in attending meetings.

Members of the Liaison Committee shall elect a chairperson from among the members serving on the committee.

12 U.S.C. § 3307. Administration

(a) Authority of Chairman of Council

The Chairman of the Council is authorized to carry out and to delegate the authority to carry out the internal administration of the Council, including the appointment and supervision of employees and the distribution of business among members, employees, and administrative units.

(b) Use of personnel, services, and facilities of Federal financial institutions regulatory agencies, Federal Reserve banks, and Federal Home Loan Banks.

[I]n addition to any other authority conferred upon it by this chapter, in carrying out its functions under this chapter, the Council may utilize, with their consent and to the extent practical, the personnel, services, and facilities of the Federal financial institutions regulatory agencies, Federal Reserve banks, and Federal Home Loan Banks, with or without reimbursement therefore.

(c) Compensation, authority, and duties of officers and employees; experts and consultants

In addition, the Council may—

(1) subject to the provisions of Title 5 relating to the competitive service, classification, and General Schedule pay rates, appoint and fix the compensation of such officers and employees as are necessary to carry out the provisions of this chapter, and to prescribe the authority and duties of such officers and employees; and

(2) obtain the services of such experts and consultants as are necessary to carry out the provisions of this chapter.

12 U.S.C. § 3308. *Access to books, accounts, records, etc., by Council*

For the purpose of carrying out this chapter, the Council shall have access to all books, accounts, records, reports, files, memorandums, papers, things, and property belonging to or in use by Federal financial institutions regulatory agencies, including reports of examination of financial institutions or their holding companies from whatever source, together with workpapers and correspondence files related to such reports, whether or not a part of the report, and all without any deletions.

12 U.S.C. § 3309. *Risk management training*

(a) Seminars

The Council shall develop and administer training seminars in risk management for its employees and the employees of insured financial institutions.

(b) Study of risk management training program

Not later than end of the 1-year period beginning on August 9, 1989, the Council shall—

(1) conduct a study on the feasibility and appropriateness of establishing a formalized risk management training program designed to lead to the certification of Risk Management Analysts; and

(2) report to the Congress the results of such study.

12 U.S.C. § 3310. *Establishment of Appraisal Subcommittee*

There shall be within the Council a subcommittee to be known as the "Appraisal Subcommittee[,"] which shall consist of the designees of the heads of the Federal financial institutions regulatory agencies, the Bureau of Consumer Financial Protection, and the Federal Housing Finance Agency. Each such designee shall be a person who has demonstrated knowledge and competence concerning the appraisal profession. At all times at least one member of the Appraisal Subcommittee shall have demonstrated knowledge and competence through licensure, certification, or professional designation within the appraisal profession.

12 U.S.C. § 3311. *Required review of regulations*

(a) In general

Not less frequently than once every 10 years, the Council and each appropriate Federal banking agency represented on the Council shall conduct a review of all regulations prescribed by the Council or by any such appropriate Federal banking agency, respectively, in order to identify outdated or otherwise unnecessary regulatory requirements imposed on insured depository institutions.

(b) Process

In conducting the review under subsection (a) of this section, the Council or the appropriate Federal banking agency shall—

(1) categorize the regulations described in subsection (a) of this section by type (such as consumer regulations, safety and soundness regulations, or such other designations as determined by the Council, or the appropriate Federal banking agency); and

(2) at regular intervals, provide notice and solicit public comment on a particular category or categories of regulations, requesting commentators to identify areas of the regulations that are outdated, unnecessary, or unduly burdensome.

(c) Complete review

The Council or the appropriate Federal banking agency shall ensure that the notice and comment period described in subsection (b)(2) of this section is conducted with respect to all regulations described in subsection (a) of this section not less frequently than once every 10 years.

(d) Regulatory response

The Council or the appropriate Federal banking agency shall—

(1) publish in the *Federal Register* a summary of the comments received under this section, identifying significant issues raised and providing comment on such issues; and

(2) eliminate unnecessary regulations to the extent that such action is appropriate.

(e) Report to Congress

Not later than 30 days after carrying out subsection (d)(1) of this section, the Council shall submit to the Congress a report, which shall include—

(1) a summary of any significant issues raised by public comments received by the Council and the appropriate Federal banking agencies under this section and the relative merits of such issues; and

(2) an analysis of whether the appropriate Federal banking agency involved is able to address the regulatory burdens associated with such issues by regulation, or whether such burdens must be addressed by legislative action.

Excerpts from Statute Governing Appraisal Subcommittee

12 U.S.C. § 3332. Functions of Appraisal Subcommittee

(a) In general

The Appraisal Subcommittee shall—

(1) monitor the requirements established by States—

(A) for the certification and licensing of individuals who are qualified to perform appraisals in connection with federally related transactions, including a code of professional responsibility; and

(B) for the registration and supervision of the operations and activities of an appraisal management company;

(2) monitor the requirements established by the Federal financial institutions regulatory agencies with respect to—

(A) appraisal standards for federally related transactions under their jurisdiction, and

(B) determinations as to which federally related transactions under their jurisdiction require the services of a State certified appraiser and which require the services of a State licensed appraiser;

(3) maintain a national registry of State certified and licensed appraisers who are eligible to perform appraisals in federally related transactions; and

(4) Omitted.

(5) transmit an annual report to the Congress not later than June 15 of each year that describes the manner in which each function assigned to the Appraisal Subcommittee has been carried out during the pre-ceding year. The report shall also detail the activities of the Appraisal Subcommittee, including the results of all audits of State appraiser regulatory agencies, and provide an accounting of disapproved actions and warnings taken in the previous year, including a description of the conditions causing the disapproval and actions taken to achieve compliance.

(6) maintain a national registry of appraisal management companies that either are registered with and subject to supervision of a State appraiser certifying and licensing agency or are operating subsidiaries of a Federally regulated financial institution.

(b) Monitoring and reviewing Foundation

The Appraisal Subcommittee shall monitor and review the practices, procedures, activities, and organizational structure of the Appraisal Foundation.

12 U.S.C. § 3333. Chairperson of Appraisal Subcommittee; term of Chairperson; meetings

(a) Chairperson

The Council shall select the Chairperson of the subcommittee. The term of the Chairperson shall be two years.

(b) Meetings; quorum; voting

The Appraisal Subcommittee shall meet in public session after notice *in the Federal Register, but may close certain portions of these meetings related to personnel and review of preliminary State audit reports*, at the call of the Chairperson or a majority of its members when there is business to be conducted. A majority of members of the Appraisal Subcommittee shall constitute a quorum but 2 or more members may hold hearings. Deci-sions of the Appraisal Subcommittee shall be made by the vote of a majority of its members. *The subject matter discussed in any closed or executive session shall be described in the Federal Register notice of the meeting.*

Excerpts from Home Mortgage Disclosure Act

12 U.S.C. § 2801. Congressional findings and declaration of purpose

(a) Findings of Congress

The Congress finds that some depository institutions have sometimes contributed to the decline of certain geographic areas by their failure pursuant to their chartering responsibilities to provide adequate home financing to qualified applicants on reasonable terms and conditions.

(b) Purpose of chapter

The purpose of this chapter is to provide the citizens and public officials of the United States with sufficient information to enable them to determine whether depository institutions are filling their obligations to serve the housing needs of the communities and neighborhoods in which they are located and to assist public officials in their determination of the distribution of public sector investments in a manner designed to improve the private investment environment.

(c) Construction of chapter

Nothing in this chapter is intended to, nor shall it be construed to, encourage unsound lending practices or the allocation of credit.

* * * * *

12 U.S.C. § 2803. Maintenance of records and public disclosure

* * *

(f) Data disclosure system; operation, etc.

The Federal Financial Institutions Examination Council, in consultation with the Secretary, shall implement a system to facilitate access to data required to be disclosed under this section. Such system shall include arrangements for a central depository of data in each primary metropolitan statistical area, metropolitan statistical area, or consolidated metropolitan statistical area that is not comprised of designated primary metropolitan statistical areas. Disclosure statements shall be made available to the public for inspection and copying at such central depository of data for all depository institutions which are required to disclose information under this section (or which are exempted pursuant to section 2805(b) of this title) and which have a home office or branch office within such primary metropolitan statistical area, metropolitan statistical area, or consolidated metropolitan statistical area that is not comprised of designated primary metropolitan statistical areas.

* * * * *

12 U.S.C. § 2809. Compilation of aggregate data

(a) Commencement; scope of data and tables

Beginning with data for calendar year 1980, the Federal Financial Institutions Examination Council shall compile each year, for each primary metropolitan statistical area, metropolitan statistical area, or consolidated metropolitan statistical area that is not comprised of designated primary metropolitan statistical areas, aggregate data by census tract for all depository institutions which are required to disclose data under section 2803 of this title or which are exempt pursuant to section 2805(b) of this title. The Council shall also produce tables indicating, for each primary metropolitan statistical area, metropolitan statistical area, or consolidated metropolitan statistical area that is not comprised of designated primary metropolitan statistical areas, aggregate lending patterns for various categories of census tracts grouped according to location, age of housing stock, income level, and racial characteristics.

(b) Staff and data processing resources

The Board shall provide staff and data processing resources to the Council to enable it to carry out the provisions of subsection (a) of this section.

(c) Availability to public

The data and tables required pursuant to subsection (a) of this section shall be made available to the public no later than December 31 of the year following the calendar year on which the data is based.

Deloitte.

Deloitte & Touche LLP
555 12ᵗʰ St. N.W.
Washington, DC 20004-1207
USA

Tel: +1 202 879 5600
Fax: +1 202 879 5309
www.deloitte.com

INDEPENDENT AUDITORS' REPORT

To the Federal Financial Institutions Examination Council:

We have audited the accompanying financial statements of the Federal Financial Institutions Examination Council (the "Council") which are comprised of the balance sheets as of December 31, 2013 and 2012, and the related statements of operations, and cash flows for the years then ended, and the related notes to the financial statements

Management's Responsibility for the Financial Statements

Management is responsible for the preparation and fair presentation of these financial statements in accordance with accounting principles generally accepted in the United States of America; this includes the design, implementation, and maintenance of internal control relevant to the preparation and fair presentation of financial statements that are free from material misstatement, whether due to fraud or error

Auditors' Responsibility

Our responsibility is to express an opinion on these financial statements based on our audits We conducted our audits in accordance with auditing standards generally accepted in the United States of America and in accordance with the standards applicable to financial audits contained in *Government Auditing Standards* issued by the Comptroller General of the United States Those standards require that we plan and perform the audit to obtain reasonable assurance about whether the financial statements are free from material misstatement An audit involves performing procedures to obtain audit evidence about the amounts and disclosures in the financial statements The procedures selected depend on the auditor's judgment, including the assessment of the risks of material misstatement of the financial statements, whether due to fraud or error In making those risk assessments, the auditor considers internal control relevant to the Council's preparation and fair presentation of the financial statements in order to design audit procedures that are appropriate in the circumstances, but not for the purpose of expressing an opinion on the effectiveness of the Council's internal control Accordingly, we express no such opinion An audit also includes evaluating the appropriateness of accounting policies used and the reasonableness of significant accounting estimates made by management, as well as evaluating the overall presentation of the financial statements

We believe that the audit evidence we have obtained is sufficient and appropriate to provide a basis for our audit opinion

Opinion

In our opinion, the financial statements referred to above present fairly, in all material respects, the financial position of the Council as of December 31, 2013 and 2012, and the results of its operations and

1

its cash flows for the years then ended in accordance with accounting principles generally accepted in the United States of America

Report on Internal Control Over Financial Reporting and on Compliance Based on an Audit of Financial Statements Performed in Accordance with Government Auditing Standards

In accordance with *Government Auditing Standards,* we have also issued our report dated February 28, 2014 on our consideration of the Council's internal control over financial reporting and on our tests of its compliance with certain provisions of laws, regulations, contracts, grant agreements and other matters The purpose of that report is to describe the scope of our testing of internal control over financial reporting and compliance and the results of that testing, and not to provide an opinion on internal control over financial reporting or compliance That report is an integral part of an audit performed in accordance with *Government Auditing Standards* in considering the Council's internal control over financial reporting and compliance

Deloitte & Touche LLP

February 28, 2014

2

FEDERAL FINANCIAL INSTITUTIONS EXAMINATION COUNCIL
Balance Sheets

	As of December 31,	
	2013	2012

ASSETS
CURRENT ASSETS:

Cash	$ 626,147	$ 638,550
Accounts receivable from member organizations	1,090,147	885,200
Accounts receivable from non-members—net	129,855	189,930
Total current assets	1,846,149	1,713,680

NONCURRENT ASSETS:

Furniture and equipment leased—net	58,231	97,929
Central Data Repository software—net	1,131,321	3,393,963
Home Mortgage Disclosure Act software—net	1,159,945	1,716,718
Total noncurrent assets	2,349,497	5,208,610
TOTAL ASSETS	$ 4,195,646	$ 6,922,290

LIABILITIES AND CUMULATIVE RESULTS OF OPERATIONS

CURRENT LIABILITIES:

Accounts payable and accrued liabilities payable to member organizations	$ 703,116	$ 840,720
Other accounts payable and accrued liabilities	700,295	484,866
Accrued annual leave	43,103	38,880
Capital lease payable	42,830	41,040
Deferred revenue	1,688,095	3,950,737
Total current liabilities	3,177,439	5,356,243

LONG-TERM LIABILITIES:

Capital lease payable	18,956	61,786
Deferred revenue	603,171	1,159,944
Deferred rent	6,783	10,085
Total long-term liabilities	628,910	1,231,815
Total liabilities	3,806,349	6,588,058
CUMULATIVE RESULTS OF OPERATIONS	389,297	334,232
TOTAL LIABILITIES AND CUMULATIVE RESULTS OF OPERATIONS	$ 4,195,646	$ 6,922,290

See notes to financial statements.

FEDERAL FINANCIAL INSTITUTIONS EXAMINATION COUNCIL
Statements of Operations

	For the years ended December 31,	
	2013	2012
REVENUES:		
Assessments on member organizations	$ 705,555	$ 687,332
Central Data Repository	5,443,813	5,398,279
Home Mortgage Disclosure Act	3,820,734	3,999,638
Tuition	3,983,198	3,605,056
Community Reinvestment Act	969,328	949,761
Uniform Bank Performance Report	359,196	396,883
Total revenues	15,281,824	15,036,949
EXPENSES:		
Data processing	4,233,290	4,392,625
Professional fees	5,109,779	4,277,394
Salaries and related benefits	2,065,455	2,023,401
Depreciation	2,859,113	3,371,828
Rental of office space	270,489	264,989
Administration fees	223,000	261,000
Travel	310,138	277,321
Other seminar expenses	46,525	22,694
Rental and maintenance of office equipment	34,097	33,612
Office and other supplies	43,695	34,145
Printing	22,416	23,561
Postage	1,585	1,419
Miscellaneous	7,177	10,123
Total expenses	15,226,759	14,994,112
RESULTS OF OPERATIONS	55,065	42,837
CUMULATIVE RESULTS OF OPERATIONS—Beginning of year	334,232	291,395
CUMULATIVE RESULTS OF OPERATIONS—End of year	$ 389,297	$ 334,232

See notes to financial statements.

FEDERAL FINANCIAL INSTITUTIONS EXAMINATION COUNCIL
Statements of Cash Flows

	For the years ended December 31,	
	2013	2012
CASH FLOWS FROM (USED IN) OPERATING ACTIVITIES:		
Results of operations	$ 55,065	$ 42,837
Adjustments to reconcile results of operations to net cash provided by operating activities:		
Depreciation	2,859,113	3,371,828
(Increase) decrease in assets:		
Accounts receivable from member organizations	(204,947)	(99,492)
Other accounts receivable	60,075	(98,410)
Increase (decrease) in liabilities:		
Accounts payable and accrued liabilities payable to member organizations	(137,603)	34,924
Other accounts payable and accrued liabilities	306,176	113,238
Accrued annual leave	4,223	15,909
Deferred revenue (current and non-current)	(2,819,416)	(2,583,162)
Deferred rent	(3,302)	89
Net cash provided by operating activities	119,384	797,761
CASH FLOWS FROM (USED IN) INVESTING ACTIVITIES:		
Capital expenditures	(88,604)	(660,365)
CASH FLOWS FROM (USED IN) FINANCING ACTIVITIES:		
Capital lease payments	(43,183)	(42,299)
NET INCREASE (DECREASE) IN CASH	(12,403)	95,097
CASH BALANCE—Beginning of year	638,550	543,453
CASH BALANCE—End of year	$ 626,147	$ 638,550

See notes to financial statements.

Notes to Financial Statements as of and for the Years Ended December 31, 2013 and 2012

1. Organization and Purpose

The Federal Financial Institutions Examination Council (the Council) was established under Title X of the Financial Institutions Regulatory and Interest Rate Control Act of 1978. The purpose of the Council is to prescribe uniform principles and standards for the federal examination of financial institutions and to make recommendations to promote uniformity in the supervision of these financial institutions. The five agencies represented on the Council during 2013, referred to collectively as member organizations, are as follows:

- Board of Governors of the Federal Reserve System (FRB)
- Consumer Financial Protection Bureau (CFPB)
- Federal Deposit Insurance Corporation (FDIC)
- National Credit Union Administration (NCUA)
- Office of the Comptroller of the Currency (OCC)

In accordance with the Financial Services Regulatory Relief Act of 2006, a representative state regulator was added as a full voting member of the Council in October 2006.

The Council was given additional statutory responsibilities by Section 340 of the Housing and Community Development Act of 1980, Public Law 96-399. Among these responsibilities are the implementation of a system to facilitate public access to data that depository institutions must disclose under the Home Mortgage Disclosure Act of 1975 (HMDA) and the aggregation of annual HMDA data, by census tract, for each metropolitan statistical area.

The Council's financial statements do not include financial data for the Council's Appraisal Subcommittee (the Subcommittee). The Subcommittee was created pursuant to Public Law 101–73, Title XI of the Financial Institutions Reform, Recovery, and Enforcement Act of 1989. Although it is a subcommittee of the Council, the Appraisal Subcommittee maintains separate financial records and administrative processes. The Council is not responsible for any debts incurred by the Appraisal Subcommittee, nor are Appraisal Subcommittee funds available for use by the Council.

2. Significant Accounting Policies

Basis of Accounting—The Council prepares its financial statements in accordance with accounting principles generally accepted in the United States (GAAP).

Revenues—Assessments are made on member organizations to fund the Council s operations based on expected cash needs. Amounts over- or under-assessed due to differences between actual and expected cash needs are presented in the "Cumulative Results of Operations" line item during the year and then may be used to offset or increase the next year's assessment. Deficits in "Cumulative Results of Operations" can be recouped in the following year's assessments.

The Council provides training seminars in the Washington, D.C. area and at locations throughout the country for member organizations and other agencies. The Council also coordinates the production and distribution of the Uniform Bank Performance Reports (UBPR) through the FDIC. Tuition and UBPR revenue are adjusted at year-end to match expenses incurred as a result of providing education classes and UBPR services. For differences between revenues and expenses, member agencies are assessed an additional amount or credited a refund based on each member's proportional cost for the Examiner Education and UBPR budget. The Council recognizes revenue from member agencies for expenses incurred related to the Community Reinvestment Act (CRA) processing system and the Home Mortgage Disclosure Act (HMDA) processing system. The Council also recognizes revenue from other agencies and mortgage insurance companies related to the Home Mortgage Disclosure Act.

Capital Assets—Furniture and equipment is recorded at cost less accumulated depreciation. Depreciation is calculated on a straight-line basis over the estimated useful lives of the assets, which range from four to ten years. Upon the sale or other disposition of a depreciable asset, the cost and related accumulated depreciation are removed and any gain or loss is recognized. The Central Data Repository (CDR) and the HMDA processing system, internally developed software projects, are recorded at cost.

Deferred Revenue—Deferred revenue includes cash collected and accounts receivable from member organizations to fund the development of CDR and the HMDA processing system. Revenue is recognized over the useful life of the system.

Deferred Rent—The lease for office and classroom space contains scheduled rent increases over the term of the lease. Scheduled rent increases must be considered in determining the annual rent expense to be recognized. The deferred rent represents the difference between the actual lease payments and the rent expense recognized.

Estimates—The preparation of financial statements in conformity with GAAP requires management to make estimates and assumptions that affect the reported amounts of assets and liabilities and the disclosure of contingent assets and liabilities at the date of the financial statements and the reported amounts of revenues and expenses during the reporting period. Actual results could differ from those estimates.

Allowance for Doubtful Accounts—Accounts receivable for non-members are shown net of the allowance for doubtful accounts. Accounts receivable considered uncollectible are charged against the allowance account in the year they are deemed uncollectible. The allowance for doubtful accounts is adjusted monthly, based upon a review of outstanding receivables.

3. Transactions with Member Organizations

	2013	2012
Accounts Receivable:		
Board of Governors of the Federal Reserve System	$ 326,875	$ 211,061
Consumer Financial Protection Bureau	31,371	42,253
Federal Deposit Insurance Corporation	364,244	268,871
National Credit Union Administration	33,624	42,370
Office of the Comptroller of the Currency	334,033	320,645
	$ 1,090,147	$ 885,200
Accounts Payable and Accrued Liabilities:		
Board of Governors of the Federal Reserve System	$ 442,749	$ 545,770
Consumer Financial Protection Bureau	3,824	5,397
Federal Deposit Insurance Corporation	143,440	161,700
National Credit Union Administration	20,087	28,470
Office of the Comptroller of the Currency	93,016	99,383
	$ 703,116	$ 840,720
Operations:		
Council operating expenses reimbursed by members	$ 705,555	$ 687,332
FRB-provided administrative support	$ 223,000	$ 261,000
FRB-provided data processing	$ 4,233,290	$ 4,392,625

The Council does not directly employ personnel, but rather member organizations detail personnel to support Council operations. These personnel are paid through the payroll systems of member organizations. Salaries and fringe benefits, including retirement benefit plan contributions, are reimbursed to these organizations. The Council does not have any post-retirement or post-employment benefit liabilities since Council personnel are included in the plans of the member organizations.

Notes continue on the following page.

Member organizations are not reimbursed for the costs of personnel who serve as Council members and on the various task forces and committees of the Council. The value of these contributed services is not included in the accompanying financial statements.

4. Central Data Repository (CDR)

In 2003, the Council entered into an agreement with UNISYS to enhance the methods and systems used to collect, validate, process, and distribute Call Report information used by member organizations, and to store this information in CDR. CDR was placed into service in October 2005. At that time, the Council began depreciating CDR on the straight-line basis over its estimated useful life of 63 months. In 2009, the Council reevaluated the useful life of CDR and decided to extend the estimated useful life by an additional 36 months based on enhanced functionality of the software. In 2013, the Council again reevaluated the useful life of CDR and decided to extend the estimated useful life by an additional 12 months. The change in estimate reduced the revenue and depreciation expense by $1,131,000 in 2013, and is expected to increase the revenue and depreciation expense in 2014 by the same amount. The Council records depreciation expenses and recognizes the same amount of revenue. The Council also pays for hosting and maintenance expenses for CDR and recognizes the associated revenue from members.

Capital Asset CDR	2013	2012
Beginning balance	$21,151,575	$20,120,566
Software placed in use during the year	0	1,031,009
Total asset	$ 21,151,575	$ 21,151,575
Less accumulated depreciation	(20,020,254)	(17,757,612)
Central Data Repository software—net	$ 1,131,321	$ 3,393,963

Accounts Payable and Accrued Liabilities Related to CDR

	2013	2012
Payable to UNISYS for the CDR project	$ 601,173	$ 219,762

CDR *Financial Activity*—The Council is funding the project by billing the three participating Council member organizations (FRB, FDIC, and OCC). Activity for the years ended December 31, 2013 and 2012, is as follows:

	2013	2012
Deferred Revenue		
Beginning balance	$ 3,393,963	$ 5,138,312
Additions	0	1,031,009
Less revenue recognized	(2,262,642)	(2,775,358)
Ending balance	$ 1,131,321	$ 3,393,963
Current portion deferred revenue	$ 1,131,321	$ 3,393,963
Long-term deferred revenue	0	0
Total Deferred Revenue	$ 1,131,321	$ 3,393,963

Total CDR Revenue		
Deferred revenue recognized	$ 2,262,642	$ 2,775,358
Hosting and maintenance revenue	3,181,171	2,622,921
Total CDR Revenue	$ 5,443,813	$ 5,398,279

Depreciation		
Depreciation for the CDR project	$ 2,262,642	$ 2,775,358

5. Home Mortgage Disclosure Act (HMDA)

FRB provides maintenance and support for the HMDA processing system. In 2007, the Council began a rewrite of the entire HMDA processing system, which went into service in 2011. At that time, the Council began depreciating the system on the straight-line basis over its estimated useful life of 60 months. The Council records depreciation expenses and recognizes the same amount of revenue each year. The Council also pays for maintenance expenses for the HMDA processing system and recognizes the associated revenue from the members and non-members. The financial activity associated with the processing system for the years ended December 31, 2013 and 2012 is as follows:

Capital asset HMDA	2013	2012
Beginning balance	$ 2,783,868	$ 2,783,868
Total asset	$ 2,783,868	$ 2,783,868
Less accumulated depreciation	(1,623,923)	(1,067,150)
HMDA software—net	$ 1,159,945	$ 1,716,718

	2013	2012
Deferred Revenue		
Beginning balance	$ 1,716,718	$ 2,273,492
Additions	0	0
Less revenue recognized	(556,773)	(556,774)
Ending balance	$ 1,159,945	$ 1,716,718
Current portion deferred revenue	$ 556,774	$ 556,774
Long-term deferred revenue	603,171	1,159,944
Total Deferred Revenue	$ 1,159,945	$ 1,716,718

Total HMDA Revenue

The Council recognized the following revenue from:

	2013	2012
Member organizations for the production and distribution of reports under the HMDA (includes the deferred revenue recognized in 2013)	$ 2,987,385	$ 3,111,398
Department of Housing and Urban Development s participation in the HMDA project	514,104	546,809
Mortgage insurance companies for HMDA-related work	319,245	341,431
Total HMDA Revenue	$ 3,820,734	$ 3,999,638

Depreciation		
Depreciation for the HMDA Rewrite project	$ 556,773	$ 556,774

6. Leases

Capital Leases—In December 2009 and November 2010, the Council entered into capital leases for printing equipment. Furniture and equipment consists of $198,485 for the capital leases as of December 31, 2013. Accumulated depreciation was $140,254 and

Notes continue on the following page.

$100,556 for 2013 and 2012, respectively. The depreciation expense for the printing equipment was $39,697 for 2013 and for 2012. Contingent rentals for excess usage of the printing equipment amounted to $18,668 and $20,544 in 2013 and 2012, respectively.

The future minimum lease payments required under the capital leases and the present value of the net minimum lease payments as of December 31, 2013 are as follows:

Years ending December 31,	Amount
2014	$ 59,089
2015	31,738
Total minimum lease payments	90,827
Less amount representing maintenance	(27,704)
Net minimum lease payments	63,123
Less amount representing interest	(1,337)
Net minimum lease payments	61,786
Less current maturities of capital lease payments	(42,830)
Long-term capital lease obligations	$ 18,956

Operating Leases — The Council entered into an operating lease with the FDIC in January 2010 to secure office and classroom space. Minimum annual payments under the operating lease having initial or remaining non-cancelable lease term of one year at December 31, 2013, are as follows:

Years ending December 31,	Amount
2014	$ 271,772
Total minimum lease payments	$ 271,772

Rental expenses under this operating lease were $264,989 for 2013 and 2012.

7. Subsequent Events

There were no subsequent events that require adjustments to or disclosures in the financial statements as of December 31, 2013. Subsequent events were evaluated through February 28, 2014, which is the date the financial statements were available to be issued.

Deloitte.

Deloitte & Touche LLP
555 12th St. N.W.
Washington, DC 20004-1207
USA

Tel: +1 202 879 5600
Fax: +1 202 879 5309
www.deloitte.com

INDEPENDENT AUDITORS' REPORT ON INTERNAL CONTROL OVER FINANCIAL REPORTING AND ON COMPLIANCE AND OTHER MATTERS BASED ON AN AUDIT OF FINANCIAL STATEMENTS PERFORMED IN ACCORDANCE WITH GOVERNMENT AUDITING STANDARDS

To the Federal Financial Institutions Examination Council:

We have audited, in accordance with the auditing standards generally accepted in the United States of America and the standards applicable to financial audits contained in *Government Auditing Standards* issued by the Comptroller General of the United States, the financial statements of the Federal Financial Institutions Examination Council (the "Council"), as of and for the years ended December 31, 2013 and 2012, and the related notes to the financial statements, and have issued our report thereon dated February 28, 2014

Internal Control Over Financial Reporting

In planning and performing our audit of the financial statements, we considered the Council's internal control over financial reporting ("internal control") to determine the audit procedures that are appropriate in the circumstances for the purpose of expressing our opinion on the financial statements, but not for the purpose of expressing an opinion on the effectiveness of the Council's internal control Accordingly, we do not express an opinion on the effectiveness of the Council's internal control

A *deficiency in internal control* exists when the design or operation of a control does not allow management or employees, in the normal course of performing their assigned functions, to prevent, or detect and correct, misstatements on a timely basis A *material weakness* is a deficiency, or a combination of deficiencies, in internal control, such that there is a reasonable possibility that a material misstatement of the entity's financial statements will not be prevented, or detected and corrected on a timely basis A *significant deficiency* is a deficiency, or a combination of deficiencies, in internal control that is less severe than a material weakness, yet important enough to merit attention by those charged with governance

Our consideration of internal control was for the limited purpose described in the first paragraph of this section and was not designed to identify all deficiencies in internal control that might be material weaknesses or significant deficiencies Given these limitations, during our audit we did not identify any deficiencies in internal control that we consider to be material weaknesses However, material weaknesses may exist that have not been identified

Compliance and Other Matters

As part of obtaining reasonable assurance about whether the Council's financial statements are free from material misstatement, we performed tests of its compliance with certain provisions of laws, regulations, contracts, and grant agreements, noncompliance with which could have a direct and material effect on the determination of financial statement amounts However, providing an opinion on compliance with those

13

provisions was not an objective of our audit, and accordingly, we do not express such an opinion The results of our tests disclosed no instances of noncompliance or other matters that are required to be reported under *Government Auditing Standards.*

Purpose of this Report

The purpose of this report is solely to describe the scope of our testing of internal control and compliance and the results of that testing, and not to provide an opinion on the effectiveness of the entity's internal control or on compliance This report is an integral part of an audit performed in accordance with *Government Auditing Standards* in considering the Council's internal control and compliance Accordingly, this communication is not suitable for any other purpose

Deloitte r Touche LLP

February 28, 2014

APPENDIX C: MAPS OF AGENCY REGIONS AND DISTRICTS

BOARD OF GOVERNORS OF THE FEDERAL RESERVE SYSTEM

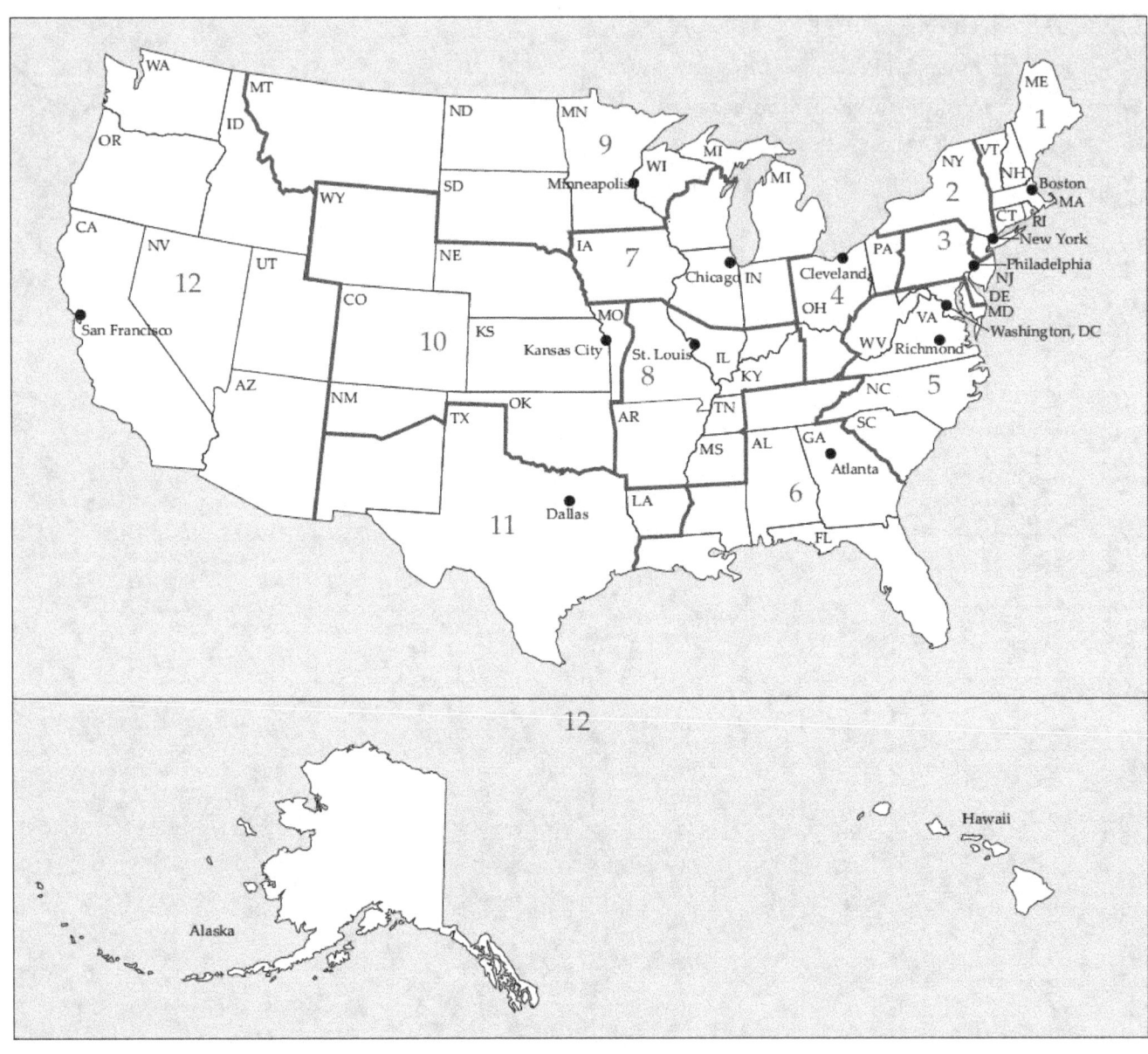

CONSUMER FINANCIAL PROTECTION BUREAU

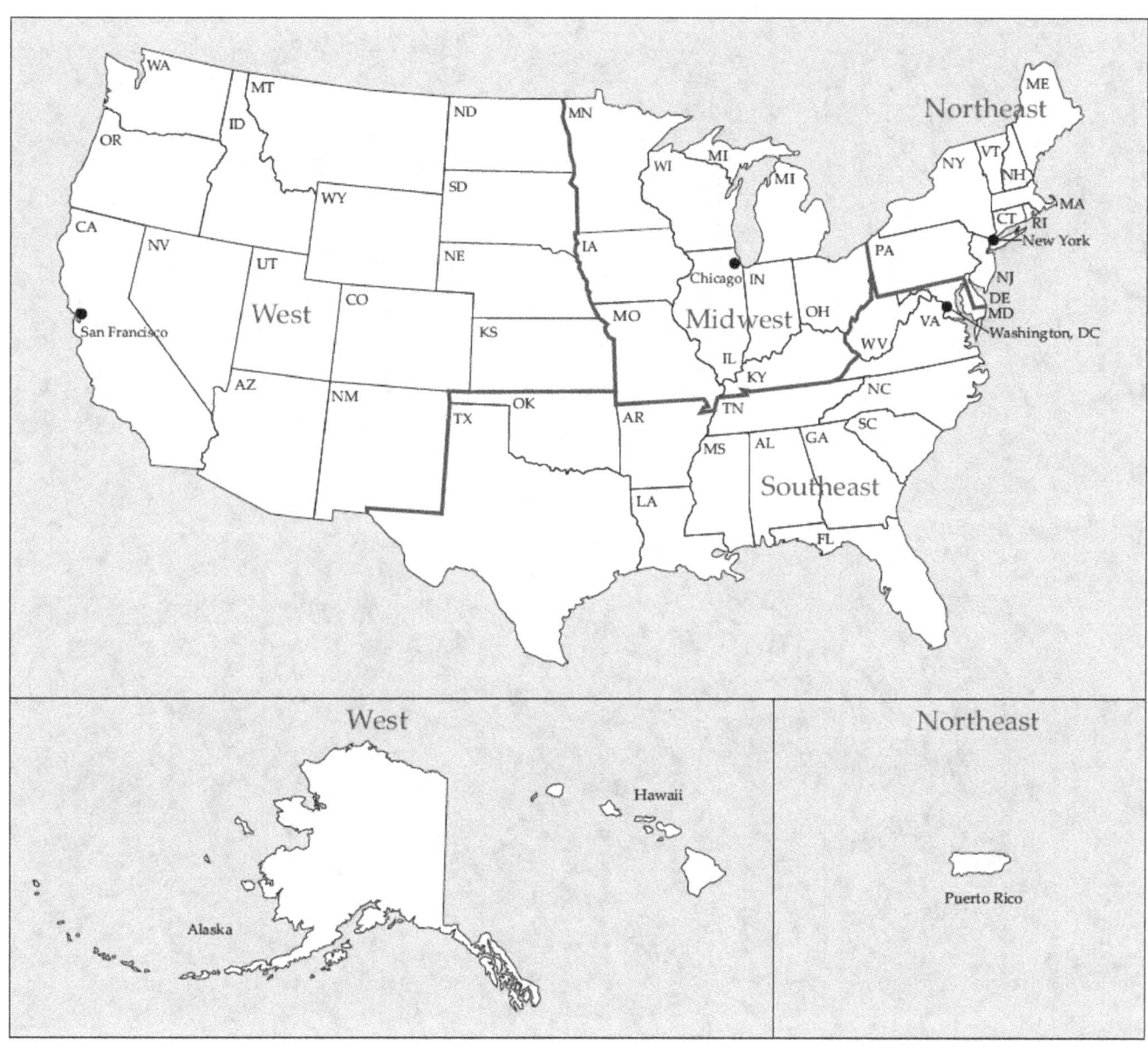

FEDERAL DEPOSIT INSURANCE CORPORATION REGIONS (SUPERVISION AND COMPLIANCE)

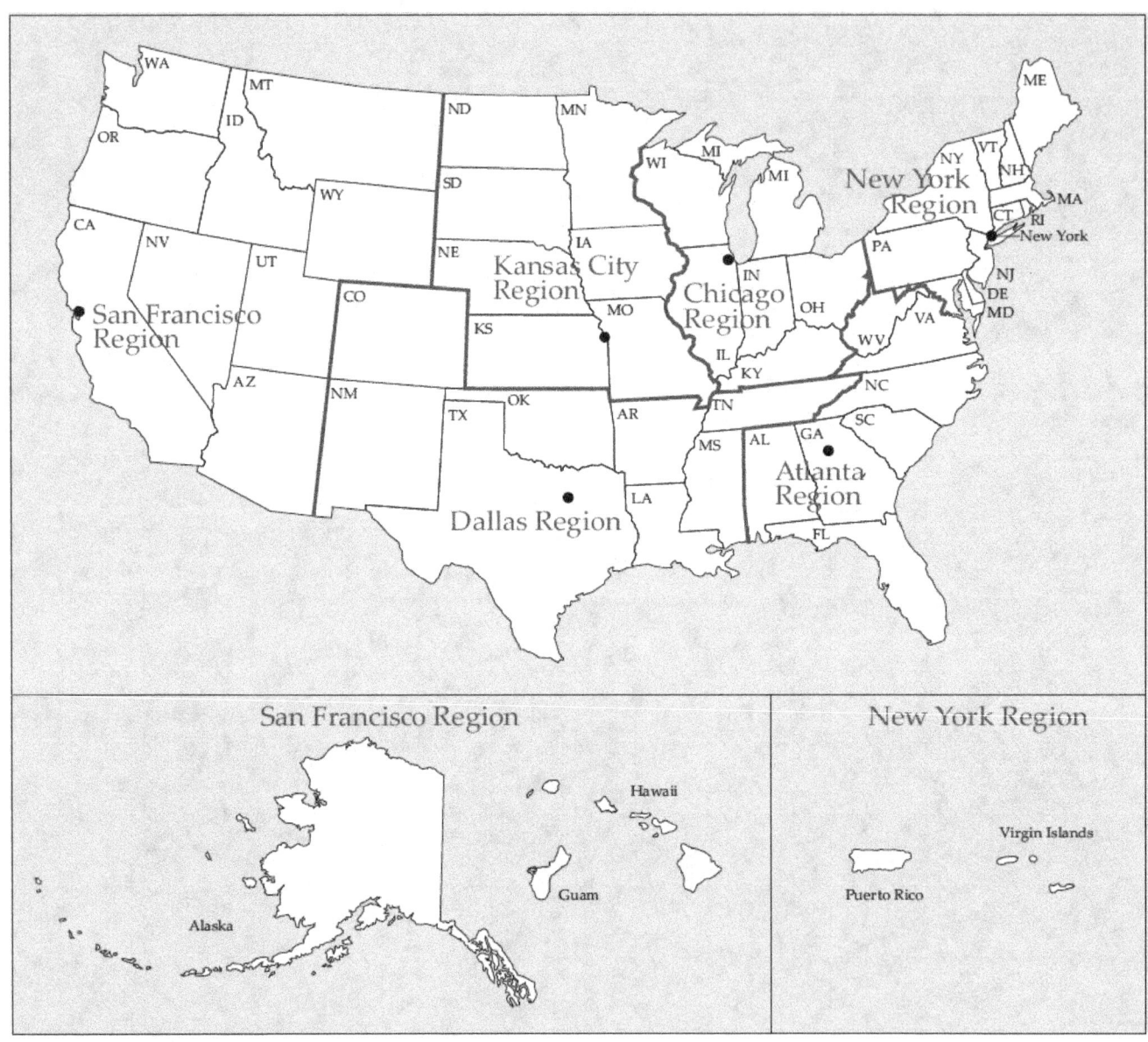

San Francisco Region

New York Region

* Two area offices are located in Boston (reports to New York) and Memphis (reports to Dallas)

NATIONAL CREDIT UNION ADMINISTRATION

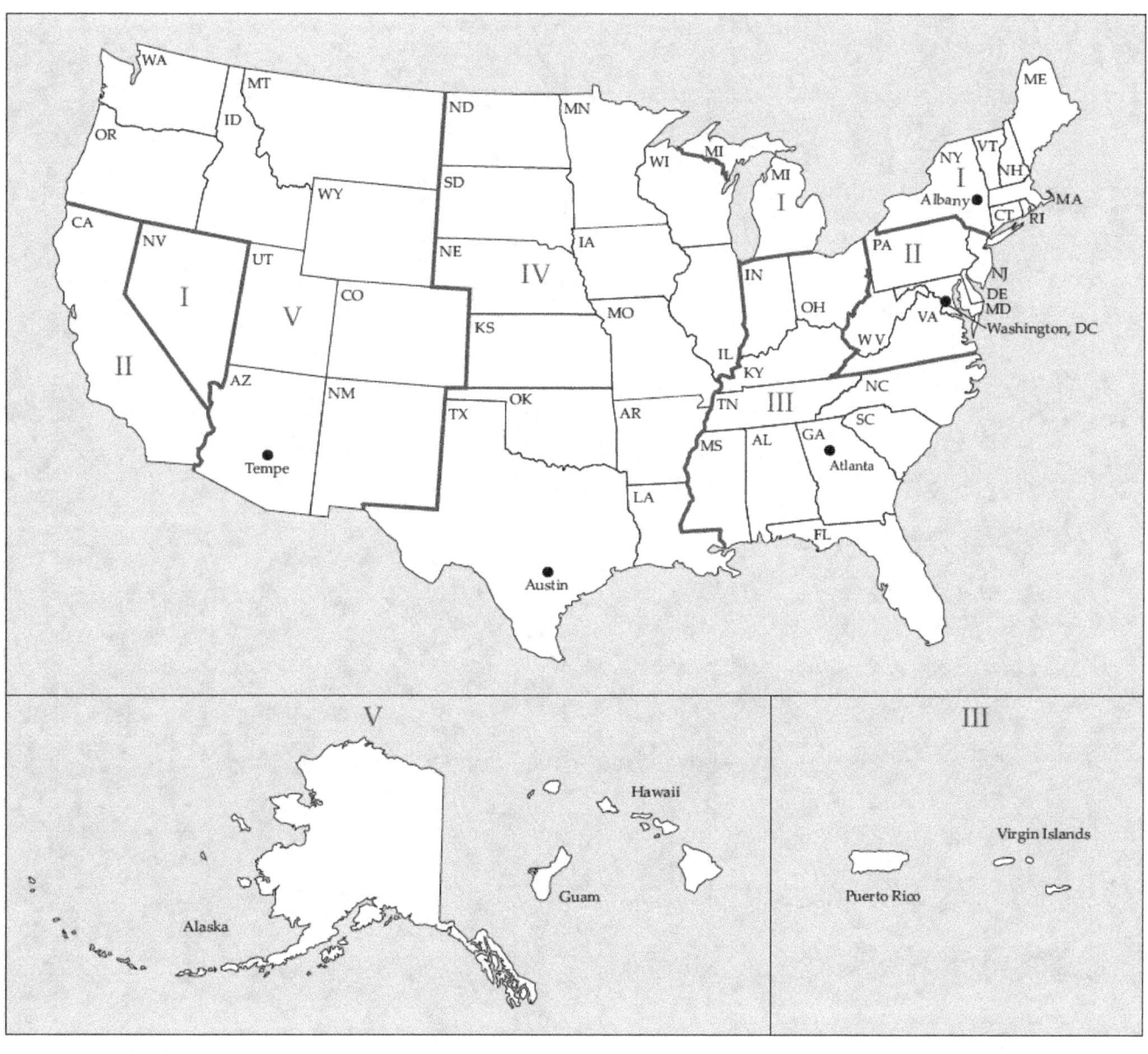

APPENDIX D: ORGANIZATIONAL LISTING OF PERSONNEL

Organization, December 31, 2013

Members of the Council

Thomas J. Curry, *Chairman*
Comptroller of the Currency
Office of the Comptroller of the Currency (OCC)

Daniel K. Tarullo, *Vice Chairman*
Member
Board of Governors of the Federal Reserve System (FRB)

Martin J. Gruenberg
Chairman
Federal Deposit Insurance Corporation (FDIC)

Richard Cordray
Director
Consumer Financial Protection Bureau (CFPB)

Debbie Matz
Chairman
National Credit Union Administration (NCUA)

David J. Cotney
Chairman
State Liaison Committee (SLC)
Commissioner of Banks
Commonwealth of Massachusetts

State Liaison Committee (SLC)

David J. Cotney, *Chairman*
Commissioner of Banks
Commonwealth of Massachusetts

Thomas Candon
De uty Commissioner
Banking and Securities
Vermont Department of Financial Regulation

Lauren Kingry
Superintendent
Arizona Department of Financial Institutions

Michael Mach
Administrator
Division of Banking
Wisconsin Department of Financial Institutions

Karen K. Lawson
Director
Office of Banking
Michigan Department of Insurance and Financial Services

Council Staff Officer

Judith E. Dupre
Executive Secretary

Interagency Staff Groups

Agency Liaison Group

John C. Lyons (OCC)
Arthur W. Lindo (FRB)
Doreen R. Eberley (FDIC)
Steven L. Antonakes (CFPB)
Larry Fazio (NCUA)
Mary Beth Quist (SLC Representative/CSBS)

Legal Advisory Group

Amy S. Friend, *Chairman* (OCC)
Scott Alvarez (FRB)
Richard J. Osterman, Jr. (FDIC)
Meredith Fuchs (CFPB)
Michael J. McKenna (NCUA)
Margaret Liu (SLC Representative/CSBS)

Task Force on Consumer Compliance

April Breslaw, *Chairman* (CFPB)
Luke H. Brown (FDIC)
Carmine Costa (SLC Representative/Connecticut)
Carol Evans (FRB)
Grovetta N. Gardineer (OCC)
Moisette I. Green (NCUA)

Task Force on Examiner Education

Philip D. Mento, *Chairman* (FDIC)
Norbert Cieslack (FRB)
Charlotte Corley (SLC Representative/Mississippi)
JeanMarie Komyathy (NCUA)
Mira Marshall (CFPB)
Thomas E. Rollo (OCC)

Task Force on Information Sharing

Jami Blume, *Chairman* (CFPB)
John Kolhoff (SLC Representative/Michigan)
Michael Kraemer (FRB)
Todd Roscoe (NCUA)
Robin Stefan (OCC)
Terrie Templemon (FDIC)

Task Force on Reports

Robert F. Storch, *Chairman* (FDIC)
Robert T. Maahs (FRB)
Kathy K. Murphy (OCC)
Elsie H. Meyer (SLC Representative/Iowa)
Ece Yolas Onat (CFPB)
Virginia L. Phillips (NCUA)

Task Force on Supervision

Doreen R. Eberley, *Chairman* (FDIC)
Steven L. Antonakes (CFPB)
Michael S. Gibson (FRB)
John C. Lyons (OCC)
D. Scott Neat (NCUA)
Charles A. Vice (SLC Representative/Kentucky)

Task Force on Surveillance Systems

Robin Stefan, *Chairman* (OCC)
Abhishek Agarwal (CFPB)
Charles W. Collier (FDIC)
Matt Mattson (FRB)
Kyle Thomas (SLC Representative/CSBS)
Kim Tuttle (NCUA)